THE
GREAT
MICROWAVE
DESSERT
COOKBOOK

THE
GREAT
MICROWAVE
DESSERT
COOKBOOK
THELMA PRESSMAN

CONTEMPORARY
BOOKS, INC.
CHICAGO

Library of Congress Cataloging-in-Publication Data

Pressman, Thelma.
    The great microwave dessert cookbook.

    Includes index.
    1. Microwave cookery.   2. Desserts.   I. Title.
TX832.P713   1985   641.8'6   85-19518
ISBN 0-8092-5277-5

Copyright © 1985 by Thelma Pressman
All rights reserved
Published by Contemporary Books, Inc.
180 North Michigan Avenue, Chicago, Illinois 60601
Manufactured in the United States of America
Library of Congress Catalog Card Number:
International Standard Book Number: 0-8092-5277-5

Published simultaneously in Canada by Beaverbooks, Ltd.
195 Allstate Parkway, Valleywood Business Park
Markham, Ontario L3R 4T8 Canada

This book is dedicated to my adored family.
If it were not for them,
whom would I have practiced on all these years?

CONTENTS

ACKNOWLEDGMENTS

My everlasting gratitude goes to Editorial Director Nancy Crossman for making it all happen: for her nurturing attitude, kind support, intelligent counseling, and, above all, for treating the microwave as it deserves to be treated—as a great piece of equipment for those of us who enjoy fresh ingredients, cooked to perfection for everyday dining, with a minimum of time and effort.

In a fortunate turn of events, my husband's new schedule made it possible for him to assist me with the recipe testing for this book. I not only welcomed the opportunity; I could not have done it without him.

It was interesting to watch Mo react with amazement when a carefully (we assumed) thought out recipe adaptation bombed. It may have tasted good, but looked as though it was made by a group of kindergarten children, or it tasted awful and looked great! We had the most interesting garbage on the block for many months. When we had a winner to add to the book, it was an achievement to relish—literally! My only problem with this entire arrangement was watching my waistline increase, while this man with his incredible inherited metabolism never gained an ounce—and never missed a bite. Welcome to the food world, Mo.

My gratitude to my beautiful niece, Noreen Barry, who brought her talent and love for creating into my test kitchen and gave it her personal touch!

Teri Sandison, a young, talented photographer, has been a wonderful source of inspiration. Working in her studio is a joy because she brings out the best in everyone, and her ability to translate her feeling for beauty into the photography of food is an experience I shall always treasure.

My deepest thanks and admiration to Jean Carey, food stylist extraordinaire, whose remarkable artistic ability is matched only by her quiet brand of subtle humor. In her capable hands, foods are transformed into works of art.

In the many years I have worked in the microwave industry, the most rewarding task has been my work with Sanyo Electric Inc. As Director of Consumer Education for Sanyo, I have the opportunity to become involved with cookbook development and education and to deal directly with the consumer and new product development. With so much happening in new technology in the kitchen, being associated with a company dedicated to excellence makes my test kitchen an exciting and progressive place to work. We all have much to look forward to—the best is yet to come.

PREFACE

Cooking equipment has come a long way since cooks placed a hand above the cast-iron top of a wood-burning stove to judge whether it was just the right temperature for the cake they had just stirred together. No one in her right mind would want to go back to that era, yet we tend to stick with what is comfortable, what we grew up with in our kitchens, and what does not present a challenge. But unless you are fortunate enough to have a staff of servants, you may wish to join the ranks of those who love to eat, entertain, and provide their loved ones with appealing, nourishing foods the simple way—with a microwave.

In the following pages, we present a selection of old favorites, some updated, plus some new dessert recipes. Only the freshest ingredients are called for in these recipes, and you'll find that you have a great selection to choose from in our modern markets. In my travels, I visit many markets around the country, and I've discovered fresh ingredients from all parts of the world. Fresh fruits are flown in from those parts of the world where summers take place during our winters. We are about to embark on a new adventure in our supermarkets—no seasons. We can have it all! A bonus of making desserts with fresh fruits is that you can minimize the use of sugar. In many of the recipes in this book, only nature's sweetness is used, without loss of flavor or appearance.

Fresh ingredients plus the microwave add up to beautiful, luscious, simple desserts. Before you begin thumbing through the recipes, be aware that there are no smart appliances, only smart cooks. So use your imagination and your culinary experience and feel free to vary the recipes and adapt your own favorites to the microwave. Bon appetit!

THE GREAT
G R E A T
MICROWAVE
DESSERT
COOKBOOK

INTRODUCING MICROWAVE DESSERTS

In *The Art of Microwave Cooking,* I presented a cooking school in each chapter. I discussed as fully as possible all the technological factors involved in understanding microwave cookery. In this lighthearted book of delightful adventures into pastry carts, on the other hand, I have concentrated on the recipes and their ingredients. Since you are all microwave owners, I believe you have knowledge of some basics of microwave power and microwave-safe utensils. Therefore, I will not go into these matters in depth in this book. In this introductory chapter, those of you who need a refresher course or a handy reference will find tips on appropriate dessert utensils and a review of power settings. Since so many of us think of chocolate when we think of dessert, there is a wide selection of chocolate desserts in this book, and at the end of this chapter you'll find tips on the use of the microwave for chocolate. More specific information on certain types of desserts—pies, candies, etc., can be found in the introductions to the appropriate recipe chapters.

Utensils

Since I assume you know that you should always use microwave-safe utensils for microwave recipes, the individual recipes in this book do not specifically state that. However, I have recommended a particular type of utensil in each recipe.

A microwave-safe utensil is one that allows the microwaves to pass through the dish. If you are not certain that your dish is safe, here is a simple test:

Place a glass measuring cup filled with water in your microwave. Place the dish you want to test next to it, but do not allow the two to touch. Heat on high (600–700 watts) for 1 minute. At the end of that time, the water will be warm and the utensil should be cold. If the dish becomes warm, it means it is absorbing microwave energy and is not microwave-safe.

MICROWAVE UTENSILS

Utensil	Sizes and Materials	Uses
Measuring cups	1, 2, 4, and 8 cups; glass	All-purpose, sauces, candies
Pie plates	9" and 10"; glass, ceramic, porcelain, microwave plastic	All-purpose, pies
Quiche dish	9" and 10"; glass, ceramic, porcelain, microwave plastic	All-purpose, pies, tarts
Ring molds	6 cups, 12 cups; glass, ceramic, porcelain, microwave plastic	Cakes
Cake pans	8" and 9"; plastic, glass, ceramic	Layer cakes

UTENSILS

Thermometers

Candy thermometers designed for microwave use are available. They may be left inside the microwave while cooking. If you do not own one, you may use your regular candy thermometer *out of the microwave* to read temperatures.

Paper

Paper products are invaluable. Many of the paper items we have used in the microwave were not appropriate for heating with food, but we used them anyway. I am happy to report that there is now a paper towel on the market designed for use with the microwave. The product is Bounty Microwave and is manufactured by Procter and Gamble. All ingredients in this towel have been approved by the FDA for contact with food. In addition to obvious uses, paper towels are ideally suited for use as liners for baking dishes. Cakes will pop right out, and the paper simply peels off.

Plastic Covers

Designed for microwave use, plastic wrap and casserole covers (I am rather proud that I designed the first one) are the most frequently used covers, because they provide seals that assure fresh-tasting, flavorful results without dehydration. Check the package to make sure the brand of plastic wrap is recommended for microwave use. If the plastic wrap stretches and melts into the food, do not use it as it may not be a material that is compatible with food.

Microwave Power Levels: Cooking Wattages

When a recipe that is to be cooked in a conventional oven calls for a power setting of 350°F, every conventional oven made (if it is accurately calibrated) is standardized to heat to the same cooking temperature at this setting.

Unfortunately, we do not yet have the same standardization on power settings for the microwave range. A Consumer Appliance Section of the International Microwave Power Institute is working on this standardization, to be used by all microwave manufacturers. While they have agreed on a standard terminology—high is 100 percent, medium-high about 70 percent, medium about 50 percent, medium-low about 30 percent, and low about 10 percent—there is no standardization of the cooking wattages these power settings represent.

What is wrong is that not all microwave units have the same high wattage. For example, if you purchase a top-of-the-line microwave, the cooking wattage on high power is 600–700 watts. On the other hand, smaller-cavity units generally have a cooking wattage on high of about 400–500 watts. These units are becoming increasingly popular because their size permits them to go into smaller spaces. Smaller-cavity units are now also available with a high power cooking wattage of about 600 watts. So it's no longer possible to assume the high power of a microwave by its size.

Power Levels to Guide You

The table on the following page shows wattage settings compared to commonly used power levels like *high* and *medium* and percentages of power such as 100 percent and 50 percent.

The purpose of this table is to make it easy for you to take microwave recipes from magazines, cookbooks, and newspapers and use them on your microwave.

This first table identifies the terminology now being used.

POWER LEVEL CONVERSIONS

Possible Descriptive Term	Power Level	Wattage	Percentage of Power
Cook	High (or 10)	600–700 watts	100%
Roast Bake	Medium High (or 7)	400–500 watts	70%
	Medium (or 5)	300–350 watts	50%
Simmer/ Defrost	Medium Low (or 3)	200–250 watts	30%
Warm/Low Defrost	Low (or 1)	60–100 watts	10%

Know Your Microwave Range

If you do not know the actual wattage for each of the power settings on your microwave, try the following:

- First, check your care and use manual or the cookbook that came with your microwave.
- If this does not have the information, write to the manufacturer. What you should find out is: On high power (100 percent), what is the cooking wattage inside the cavity? (It can be anywhere from 400 watts to 700 watts.) On medium-high power (70 percent), what is the cooking wattage? (It can be anywhere from 300 watts to 500 watts.) And so on. Be sure to include the model number of your unit.
- If you can't get wattage information from the manufacturer, let me suggest a simple water test. Place an 8-ounce cup of cold tap water in a glass measuring cup inside your microwave range. Using high power for the first test, watch and record how long it takes for the water to come to a rolling boil. Before repeating the test for each setting, allow the microwave cavity and glass cup to cool completely.

Follow the table below to determine what your approximate wattages are at each setting.

TO DETERMINE COOKING WATTAGE AT EACH MICROWAVE POWER LEVEL

If 8 ounces of water boils within this time:	Your cooking wattage is approximately:
2½–3 minutes	600–700 watts
3½–4 minutes	400–500 watts
4½–5½ minutes	300–350 watts
8½–10 minutes	200–250 watts
does not boil	60–100 watts

Since your tap water is not always the same, do not be concerned if there are slight variations in your tests. This is not a scientific test; it is just intended to give you approximate wattages.

Once you are aware of what each power setting on your microwave is in terms of cooking wattages, you can then cook by wattage numbers.

Should you discover that your medium-high, medium, medium-low, and low cooking wattages are lower or higher than the ones I have used in my testing, you can adjust by using slightly less time or slightly more time. The difference 100 watts of cooking power makes is not too great, so do not worry if it is not exactly the same. The significant difference will be in the smaller units and in the older models, which use 50 percent of power as the defrost setting instead of 30 percent, because that was all there was in the early days.

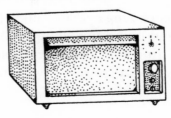

Please note: All of the recipes in this book have been developed and tested using a high power of 600–700 watts. If your range has a high power of 400–500 watts, add 30 seconds to each minute of cooking time. If your range operates on a high power of 500–600 watts, add 15 seconds to each minute of cooking time.

Each recipe in this book lists the appropriate wattage in parentheses only the *first* time each power setting is mentioned in the directions. If you have any doubts about the proper wattage when reading a recipe, refer back to the power level conversion table on page 5.

How to Use Chocolate

Whole volumes have been written about working with chocolate, which can be a tricky business indeed. Nevertheless, true chocoholics will spare no expense or effort to create their favorite desserts and confections. Well, the microwave brings good news for chocolate lovers: it's ideal for melting chocolate without the fuss. Here are some tips on making the most of chocolate in your microwave.

Terminology

Unsweetened chocolate: Known as baking, cooking, or bitter chocolate, it is intended primarily for baking. I often add it to sweetened chocolate because it adds a rich quality and cuts the sweetness.

Bittersweet chocolate: Slightly sweetened, dark chocolate, it is used for desserts, for some baking, and is the confectioner's choice for dipping.

Semisweet chocolate: Sometimes called *sweet chocolate*, it is the choice of French chefs for baking. It is also used for frosting, fillings, sauces, creams, and mousses.

Milk chocolate: America's favorite, it works best for pies, puddings, and some steamed desserts.

White chocolate: Called chocolate but has only one chocolate component—cocoa butter. It is used for mousses, frostings, fillings, and cakes and for dipping.

Compound coatings: Not real chocolate—made of a hardened vegetable fat base, they are also called "Summer Coatings." Perfect for molding, because it is easy to work with. Comes in a rainbow of colors. It was this development that made it possible for everyone to use molds at home to make their own favorite decorative shapes, without providing the unique environment so necessary for "real chocolate" molding as done by professionals.

Basic Techniques for Chocolate

(Portions of this section previously appeared in my microwave column in *Bon Appetit* magazine, October 1981.)

Chocolate varies in texture, and therefore timings may vary when it is melted. If it is "cooked" rather than melted, the damage to the quality is beyond repair—it will become grainy and hard.

For best results, microwave melting of chocolate is ideal, since you do not use direct heat underneath the pan, which could cause scorching. Just remember to look for this clue that the chocolate has softened: the chocolate will change from a dull color to a shiny surface but will *not appear melted* until you stir. Cooking is stopped before chocolate becomes runny or melted.

The recipes that call for melted chocolate use high power (600–700 watts). Once the chocolate has become shiny (a minute or two, depending on the amount), it is stirred until it melts.

Chocolate bits encourage quick melting. It is always best to break large bars into pieces or to grate the chocolate in your food processor. The smaller the pieces, the quicker the melting.

Once the chocolate is dissolved after stirring, if you need to reheat a small amount, it is best to use medium power for small periods of time. Begin with 30 seconds, stir, then add seconds of timing rather than minutes to avoid grainy chocolate.

Substitutions

For baking chocolate: 3 tablespoons cocoa plus 1 tablespoon shortening equals 1 ounce baking chocolate.

For semisweet chocolate: 6 tablespoons cocoa plus 7 tablespoons sugar plus ¼ cup solid shortening equals one 6-ounce package (1 cup) semisweet chocolate chips or 6 ounces semisweet chocolate.

For sweet cooking chcolate: 4 tablespoons cocoa plus 4⅔ tablespoons sugar plus 2⅔ tablespoons shortening equals one 4-ounce bar sweet cooking chocolate.

Chocolate Tips

The microwave cuts down hours of preparation, allows you to control temperature better, and, because of its speed, allows you to work in small, controlled quantities.

For all of the chocoholics in the world, let me assure you: you do not need to be a professional to experience good results.

- Chocolate chips, bits, or chunks will become shiny but will *not* lose their shape when "melted"—they will not melt in the traditional sense. Stir through several times with a wooden spoon until chocolate is smooth to complete melting.
- Break up chocolate into smaller pieces to speed up the softening. Use high power for small amounts. For large amounts of chocolate used with liquid, high power is

still best, since it speeds up the process. With large amounts of chocolate only, either melt in small batches or use a lower setting to avoid overheating.

- The temperature of the room is a crucial factor when you are dipping or working with melted chocolate. The ideal temperature is 65–68°F—a cool room is always better than a warm, humid room.
- Never cover chocolate when melting since it will cause moisture to form on the inside, and even one drop of moisture can cause the chocolate to ball up and stiffen.
- Although you can add a tablespoon or so of vegetable oil to melted chocolate, it will affect the texture and taste.
- A good-quality chocolate with cocoa butter retained is ideal to work with, and experimenting with different chocolate products will give you greater insight into quality and taste. Try taking the wrappers off different products and tasting each one slowly. You can then get a feeling for the differences in texture and taste. Then read the labels to understand the differences in the products. It will make it easier to judge chocolate products before purchasing large amounts.
- Problems can occur when temperature changes. It can cause chocolate to turn color, or a grayish-white mottling on the finished chocolate can occur. Although it is unattractive, it does not affect the taste.

The Ultimate Chocolate Cake
Chocolate Cake with Almond Custard Filling
Chocolate Sherry Cake
Chocolate Mousse Layer Cake
Chocolate Charlotte Russe
Cheesecake
Pineapple Honey Cake
Steamed Fresh Peach Cake
Apple Cake Marsala
Almond Layer Cake
Lemon Coconut Layer Cake
English Trifle
Zucchini Cake
Gingerbread Ring
Pumpkin Cake
Carrot Cake
Caramelized Raisin-Nut Ring

1
CAKES

It is important not to overcook cakes because that dries them out. Even though the top of the cake appears moist, it may be done. Watch the edges: the minute the cake begins to pull away from the sides slightly, it may be done. Let it cool on a flat surface, rather than a rack, which will assure that the bottom will be done as well.

There are many manufacturers making plastic cake baking dishes for microwave use. You may also use the glass round 8″ variety. It should be at least 2½ inches high. Lining the bottom of the cake dish with a circle of Bounty Microwave paper towel makes it easy to remove the cake, then peel off the towel. To cut the circle, turn the cake dish upside down and place a sheet of towel on the bottom. Cut the circle to fit the bottom of the dish and fit it inside before pouring the cake batter in.

THE ULTIMATE
CHOCOLATE CAKE

This cake was adapted from a conventional recipe, using mayonnaise as the shortening. It works extremely well in the microwave. All I changed was the timing for microwave cooking—6-8 minutes per layer instead of 35 minutes.

This is a moist, chocolaty cake, and the frosting is just the right touch. I have suggested a sprinkle of chocolate shots on the top and sides.

> **2 cups flour (all purpose)**
> **⅔ cup unsweetened cocoa powder**
> **1¼ teaspoons baking soda**
> **¼ teaspoon baking powder**
> **1⅔ cups sugar**
> **4 eggs**
> **1 tablespoon vanilla**
> **1 cup Hellmann's Real Mayonnaise**
> **1⅓ cups water**
> **The Ultimate Chocolate Frosting**
> **(see index)**

Cut circles of Bounty Microwave paper towels to fit inside baking pans, then line both bottoms of two 8″ layer cake microwave dishes.

In a bowl, mix together flour, cocoa, baking soda, and baking powder. In large mixing bowl, with mixer at high speed, beat sugar, eggs, and vanilla about 3 minutes, until light and fluffy. At low speed, beat in mayonnaise. Add flour mixture with a mixing spoon, in 4 additions, alternately with water, beginning and ending with flour. Pour into pans.

Cook on medium (300–350 watts) 4 minutes. Rotate dish if it appears to be cooking unevenly. Continue cooking on high (600–700 watts) for 3–5 minutes, just until it begins to set on the outside edges. Although the center may appear slightly soft, it will set as it cools. Allow to cool on a flat heatproof surface before inverting layers onto 10″ or 12″ plates.

Frost and fill layers with The Ultimate Chocolate Frosting.

SERVES 10–12

CHOCOLATE CAKE WITH ALMOND CUSTARD FILLING

Be very gentle when moving this delicate cake as it crumbles easily.

2 cups sugar
1¾ cups flour
¾ cup unsweetened cocoa powder
2 teaspoons baking soda
1 teaspoon baking powder
1 teaspoon salt
1 teaspoon instant coffee powder
2 eggs, room temperature
¾ cup strong coffee
¾ cup buttermilk
½ cup vegetable oil
1 teaspoon vanilla

ALMOND CUSTARD FILLING

2 eggs, room temperature
2 egg yolks
1 cup sugar
1 cup milk, scalded
¼ cup flour
3 tablespoons unsalted butter
½ cup finely chopped toasted almonds
2 teaspoons vanilla
½ teaspoon amaretto

FROSTING

¾ cup (1½ sticks) butter
1¼ cups unsweetened cocoa powder
3½ cups powdered sugar
½ cup milk
2 teaspoons vanilla

For cake: Line bottom of two 8″ round cake pans with Bounty Microwave paper towels. Combine sugar, flour, cocoa powder, baking soda, baking powder, salt, and instant coffee powder in large bowl. Combine eggs, coffee, buttermilk, oil, and vanilla in another large bowl and beat well. Add egg mixture to dry ingredients and mix thoroughly. Pour half of batter into prepared pan. Cook on high (600–700 watts), 6–6½ minutes, turning if cake begins cooking unevenly. Let cool on flat surface 10 minutes. Invert cake onto plate. Repeat with remaining batter. When cool, cut each cake in half horizontally to make four layers. Set aside.

For filling: Combine eggs, egg yolks, sugar, milk, and flour in 1-quart measure and cook on high 2 minutes. Stir through several times. Continue cooking on high 30 seconds. Repeat cooking and stirring at 30-second intervals until mixture is thick, about 2 minutes. Blend in butter. Add chopped almonds, vanilla, and amaretto and beat until smooth, about 1 minute.

For frosting: Melt butter in 2-quart measure on high 45 seconds. Stir in cocoa and cook on high 30 seconds. Let cool. Add sugar and milk alternately to mixture, beating until smooth and thick, about 3 minutes. Stir in vanilla.

To assemble: Set one cake layer on serving platter. Spread with ⅓ of filling. Top with second layer and spread with another ⅓ of filling. Add third layer and cover with remaining filling. Set fourth layer on top. Cover top and sides of cake with frosting. Serve at room temperature or chilled.

SERVES 10–12

CHOCOLATE SHERRY CAKE

Give your chocolate cake a more intriguing flavor by sprinkling with a bit of your favorite sherry, Kahlua, Chambord, or a touch of sweet wine. Then spread with your favorite frosting or whipped cream.

2 cups flour

1⅔ cups sugar

⅔ cup unsweetened cocoa powder

1 teaspoon salt

1½ teaspoons soda

½ teaspoon baking powder

1¼ cups water

¾ cup butter-flavored vegetable shortening

2 large eggs

1 tablespoon vanilla

1 tablespoon ground cinnamon

½ teaspoon ground cloves

Sherry, liqueur, or sweet wine for
  sprinkling (a few tablespoons)

Frosting for 2-layer cake (see index for
  recipes) *or* Coffee-Flavored Whipped
  Cream (see recipe below)

Cut a sheet of Bounty Microwave paper towel to fit inside each of two 8″ round microwave baking dishes. If you have only one dish, you may repeat preparation and cooking for the second layer.

In a large mixing bowl, combine the flour, sugar, cocoa, salt, soda, baking powder, water, shortening, eggs, vanilla, cinnamon, and cloves. Beat at high speed for 3 minutes. Divide batter between two 8″ baking dishes. Bake each layer on medium (300–350 watts) for 5 minutes, turning if it appears to be cooking unevenly. Then cook on high (600–700 watts) 3–5 minutes, just until outside edges begin to move away from the edges. Although center may appear slightly moist, it will set as it cools.

Place cake dishes on heatproof flat surface until they cool slightly (about 20 minutes) before inverting onto 10″ or 12″ plates. Peel off paper towels. Sprinkle each layer with wine.

Frost with your favorite frosting or with Coffee-Flavored Whipped Cream.

SERVES 8–10

COFFEE-FLAVORED WHIPPED CREAM

2 cups whipping cream
2 tablespoons Kahlua
1 tablespoon sugar

Beat cream until soft peaks form. Add Kahlua and sugar and continue beating until stiff. Frost each layer with whipped cream.

MAKES ABOUT 2 CUPS

CHOCOLATE MOUSSE LAYER CAKE

Turn a simple cake mix into a festive, sinfully rich cake that should be shared with your favorite chocoholic. (See photo.)

1 yellow cake mix (18.25 ounces)
Chocolate Almond Mousse filling
  (see index)
Solid vegetable shortening (to grease pan)

CHOCOLATE SAUCE FROSTING

1 cup sugar
½ cup light cream
4 ounces unsweetened baking chocolate
½ cup butter, cut into pieces
2 egg yolks, beaten
1 teaspoon vanilla

24 white Chocolate Leaves for garnish
  (see index)
½ cup fresh raspberries for garnish

For cake: Follow package directions for preparing cake batter. Prepare Chocolate Almond Mousse filling and set aside to cool.

Lightly grease bottom of 10″–12″ Bundt pan with solid shortening. Pour batter into pan. Cook on high (600–700 watts) for 10–11 minutes, turning pan if cake appears to be cooking unevenly. When done, cake will pull lightly away from pan. Cool slightly on flat, heat resistant surface for 10–15 minutes before inverting on serving plate. Cake will come out better if still warm.

When cooled completely, cut into three layers. Divide the mousse in half and spread thickly on each layer.

For frosting: Combine sugar and cream in a 4-cup measure. Cook on high, uncovered, 4 minutes, or until sugar dissolves and mixture boils. Add chocolate and butter. Stir to blend; cook an additional 30 seconds to 1 minute. Add half the chocolate mixture to beaten egg yolks. Stir egg yolk mixture into remaining chocolate mixture in measuring cup. Cook on medium (300-350 watts) for 2 minutes. Whisk in the vanilla.

Frost. Garnish with Chocolate Leaves and raspberries.

SERVES 12-14

CHOCOLATE CHARLOTTE RUSSE

Rich desserts seem to run in our family. When niece Siri invited us to dinner, I begged her to keep the meal light, perhaps featuring some of her famous wok cooking. She obliged. But then, like many of us, she was afraid we would not be satisfied with the light fare and prepared this sinful, rich, decadent dessert. It is so rich that it may serve even more than 16. Serve it to your favorite chocoholics. Great for a larger dinner party or special event.

> 18 ladyfingers, split
> 1 12-ounce package (2 cups) semisweet real chocolate
> 2 8-ounce packages cream cheese
> ½ cup sugar
> ¼ teaspoon salt
> 1 tablespoon vanilla
> 3 eggs, separated
> 2 cups whipping cream, whipped
> Additional whipped cream for garnish (optional)
> Chocolate Curls (optional) (see index)

Line sides of a 9″ springform pan with ladyfingers, rounded sides against pan. Line bottom of pan with remaining ladyfingers to fit.

In a 4-cup glass measure, melt chocolate on high (600–700 watts) 1½–2 minutes, just until morsels turn shiny; stir until melted. Place unwrapped cheese on a plate. Warm for 45 seconds to 1 minute at 50 percent of power to soften. In a large bowl, combine cheese, sugar, salt, vanilla, and egg yolks. Beat until light and fluffy. Add melted chocolate and set aside.

With clean beaters, in a small bowl, beat egg whites until stiff but not dry. Fold into chocolate mixture. Fold in whipped cream. Spoon into prepared springform pan. Chill until set. Remove sides of springform pan. Place on serving plate. Garnish with additional whipped cream and Chocolate Curls, if desired. Additional color may be added with a few Maraschino cherries arranged on top.

SERVES 14–16

CHEESECAKE

Once you begin to "bake" in the microwave you will enjoy using some of the simple methods of preparing old favorites, like this cheesecake.

I always cut the sugar and find my tasters enjoy the fresh flavor of the cheese without too much sweetness. If you miss it, add another ¼ cup of sugar.

The microwave plastic, glass, or ceramic 8″ round baking dish is extremely important *in creating the microwave version of layered oven-baked cakes.*

⅓ cup butter
1½ cups packaged graham cracker crumbs
   or about 12 double graham crackers,
   crushed
2 8-ounce packages cream cheese
3 eggs
½ cup sugar
1 teaspoon vanilla

TOPPING

1 cup sour cream
2-3 tablespoons confectioners' (powdered)
sugar

For cake: Melt butter on high (600–700 watts) in 8″ round baking dish 1½ minutes. Blend in crumbs and remove ¼ cup to use later. Press crumbs evenly on bottom of dish and up the sides.

Place unwrapped cheese in glass bowl. Soften on high for 1 minute. Beat until smooth and fluffy. Beat in eggs, sugar, and vanilla until smooth. Pour into the baking dish and cook on medium (300–350 watts) 3 minutes to set cake. Raise power level to high (600–700 watts) for 5–7 minutes, turning dish if it appears to be cooking unevenly. Center will not be set when cake is done, but it will become firm as cheesecake cools.

For topping: Combine sour cream and sugar for the topping and stir to blend. Set aside while cake is cooling.

When cake has cooled, spoon on topping and sprinkle reserved crumbs around the edge of the cake and a touch in the center. Refrigerate until ready to serve.

May be served with fresh blueberries and whipped cream.

SERVES 6

PINEAPPLE HONEY CAKE

The carrots and pineapple give moisture and color—an outstanding flavor.

¾ cup salad oil
½ cup honey
2 eggs
1 cup finely shredded carrots

1 4-ounce can crushed pineapple
  (including juice)
1⅓ cups whole wheat flour
1 teaspoon baking soda
1 teaspoon ground cinnamon
1 teaspoon baking powder
¼ teaspoon ground ginger
½ cup chopped walnuts
Cream Cheese Icing (optional)
  (see recipe below)

In a medium-size mixing bowl, mix together on low speed oil, honey, eggs, carrots, and the pineapple with juice. Stir in remaining ingredients. Pour into a glass or ceramic loaf pan (8½″ × 6″). Cook on medium (300–350 watts) for 6 minutes. Turn and cook for 6 minutes on medium high (400–500 watts), until a cake tester comes out dry. Let cool. Top with Cream Cheese Icing, if desired.

SERVES 6

CREAM CHEESE ICING

1 3-ounce package cream cheese
¼ cup honey
2 teaspoons vanilla
1 teaspoon cornstarch
1 tablespoon water

In small bowl, heat cream cheese and honey for 30 seconds to 1 minute on high (600–700 watts), until the mixture is softened. Stir until smooth. Dissolve cornstarch in vanilla and water. Add to mixture and stir. Beat for 30 seconds or until slightly thickened. Frost the cooled cake.

MAKES ABOUT ½ CUP

STEAMED FRESH PEACH CAKE

This is a good Bundt cake. Many years ago this technique was developed to work with a 6-cup Bundt or ring mold and a 2-quart shallow casserole with a rack that fit into the casserole and a large bubble-type cover for the top.

> 1 cup fresh peach pulp (or other fresh fruit pulp), from about 4 ripe peaches, unpeeled, stones removed, processed in food processor or blender
> 2 teaspoons baking soda
> ½ cup butter
> 1 cup sugar
> 2 eggs
> 2 tablespoons water
> 1 teaspoon vanilla
> 1 cup flour
> 1 teaspoon ground cinnamon
> ¼ teaspoon ground nutmeg
> ¼ teaspoon ground allspice
> ½ cup chopped pecans
> 1 cup raisins

BRANDY SAUCE

1 cup sugar
½ cup (1 stick) butter
4 egg yolks, well beaten
1 cup whipping cream
2–3 tablespoons brandy

For cake: Blend the peach pulp with soda and set aside. Cream together the butter and sugar. Add eggs, water, and vanilla and beat until blended.

Combine dry ingredients. Blend dry ingredients into creamy mixture. Stir in peach pulp, nuts, and raisins and blend thoroughly.

Pour batter into greased 6-cup Bundt or ring mold. Place on microwave rack over ½ inch boiling water and cover with tight lid. Cook on high (600–700 watts) for 10–11 minutes or until long pick comes out clean. Let stand 15 minutes before unmolding.

For sauce: Cream together the sugar and butter. Add egg yolks and cream and beat well. Cook on medium (300–350 watts) until mixture thickens slightly, stirring twice, about 5–6 minutes. Add the brandy to taste. Serve cake warm with sauce. Flame with brandy if desired.

SERVES 6–8

APPLE CAKE MARSALA

2–3 red baking apples
¼ pound (1 stick) butter
¾ cup sugar
Grated rind of 1 small lemon
2 eggs, slightly beaten
1¼ cups flour
1½ teaspoons baking powder
¼ cup milk
3 tablespoons marsala
  (may substitute sherry)

GLAZE

½ cup apple jelly
1 teaspoon ground cinnamon

For cake: Core and thinly slice apples. (The red skin on the apple adds color.) Beat butter until smooth. Add sugar, lemon rind, and eggs and mix well.

Add flour, baking powder, milk, and sherry and mix just until blended.

Spread batter with a spatula (it will be thick) into a 9″ pie plate. Arrange apple slices, sunburst fashion, on batter. Press each slice gently in place.

Bake on medium (300–350 watts) for 4 minutes, turning cake if it appears to be cooking unevenly. Continue to bake on high (600–700 watts) for 2–3 minutes, rotating once or twice if it appears to be cooking unevenly. (Remember, top will not brown.) Allow to stand at least 10 minutes. Wet spots on top will evaporate.

For glaze: Melt jelly on high in small dish 30–40 seconds. Stir in cinnamon. Use a pastry brush and brush glaze over cake. Allow to set and serve.

SERVES 6–8

ALMOND LAYER CAKE

This beautifully decorated layer cake, featured on our cover, was prepared from a simple cake mix using a microwave technique to produce a delightfully fresh treat. (See photo.)

> 1 yellow cake mix (18.25 ounces)
> 2 tablespoons butter
> 2 cups sliced almonds

FRUIT GARNISH AND FILLING

½ pint whipping cream (2 cups whipped)
2 cups sliced fruit
¼ cup apple jelly

For cake: Follow package directions for preparing cake batter and set aside.

In glass pie plate, melt butter on high (600–700 watts) for 1 minute. Stir in almonds until coated. Cook on high 2–3 minutes, or until toasted, stirring twice. Set aside until cool. Place almonds in food processor or blender and chop into coarse pieces.

Prepare two 8″ layer cake dishes, buttering bottom and sides liberally. Sprinkle bottom and sides with equal portions of almonds (1 cup each pan). Pour half of cake batter into each dish. Cook on high about 6 minutes, just until cake begins to pull away from sides of pan (top will still be moist but will firm up as it cools). Turn dish if cake appears to be cooking unevenly.

Cool on a heat-resistant, flat surface (do not use wire racks). Allow to cool for 10–15 minutes before inverting on plate.

For garnish and filling: While cake cools, heat apple jelly on high 45 seconds. When cool, frost the bottom layer with whipped cream and fruit of your choosing. Arrange fruit in a sunburst pattern on top layer (see cover), brush glaze over fruit, and garnish with whipped cream.

SERVES 8–10

LEMON COCONUT LAYER CAKE

A fresh-tasting yellow cake from a mix, with a white coconut frosting made light and airy with egg whites.

1 lemon cake mix (18.50 ounces)
2 teaspoons grated fresh lemon rind
1 teaspoon lemon juice
½ cup finely chopped shredded coconut

FROSTING

1 cup sugar
½ cup water
Dash salt
2 egg whites
¼ teaspoon cream of tartar
1 teaspoon vanilla
1 cup shredded coconut

For cake: Prepare cake mix according to package directions. Fold in lemon rind, lemon juice, and ½ cup shredded coconut. Divide evenly between two lightly greased (using solid shortening) 8″ microwave cake pans. (If you own only one pan, do one at a time.)

Cook on high (600–700 watts) for 3 minutes. Reduce cooking power to medium (300–350 watts) for 3–5 minutes, just until cake begins to move slightly away from the sides. During cooking, turn pan if cake appears to be cooking unevenly. Center may still be slightly moist but will set as it cools. Place dish on a solid surface rather than a rack to cool. This will trap the heat and give better final results.

For frosting: Combine sugar, water, and salt in 2-cup glass measure. Cook on high 3–4 minutes, stir until sugar dissolves. In small mixing bowl, beat egg whites and cream of tartar until soft peaks form. Gradually add hot syrup mixture to egg whites, beating constantly. Continue beating for 5 minutes, or until mixture is thick and fluffy. It is important not to underbeat. Beat in vanilla.

Frost top of first layer and sprinkle with coconut. Place second layer on top and frost top and sides of both layers. Sprinkle top and sides with remaining coconut.

SERVES 8

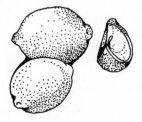

ENGLISH TRIFLE

The story goes that an enterprising chef in a large English hotel, concerned about waste of food, designed a way to "recycle" day-old cake by freshening the stale cake with sherry, spreading it with jam to give it flavor, and alternating layers with layers of custard.

What makes our recipe special is the fresh taste of the homemade raspberry sauce. You can certainly use the same technique with instant custards and prepared jams, but it will never bring the raves this freshly prepared trifle elicits.

Make the sauce first so that it will have time to cool slightly, then prepare the custard. The trifle is best when made on the day it is served. (See photo.)

RASPBERRY SAUCE

1 12-ounce package frozen raspberries
½ cup currant jelly
2 tablespoons cornstarch
2 tablespoons Chambord
  (raspberry liqueur) or water

CUSTARD

½ cup cornstarch   4 egg yolks, lightly beaten
4 cups milk   1 tablespoon butter
1 scant cup sugar   2 teaspoons vanilla
⅛ teaspoon salt

FOR ASSEMBLY OF TRIFLE

1 pound good-quality pound cake (look in
  your supermarket's frozen cake section)
2 packages ladyfingers (15–20 cakes)
¼ cup cream sherry
½ cup sliced almonds
Whipped cream for garnish

For sauce: Place raspberries in 1-quart glass measure. Cook on high (600–700 watts) 2–3 minutes, just until defrosted. (Timing will depend on how solidly frozen the fruit is when taken out of the package.) Stir in currant jelly and continue to cook on high 1–2 minutes, until it comes to a boil. Combine cornstarch and Chambord or water and stir until cornstarch is completely dissolved. Stir into raspberries and continue to cook on high until mixture thickens and clears, about 2–3 minutes. Set aside to cool.

For custard: Place cornstarch in a 2-quart glass measure or bowl, add 1 cup of the milk, and stir until cornstarch is completely dissolved. Blend in sugar, salt, and remaining milk. Cook on high 8–12 minutes or until thickened, stirring every 3 minutes. Stir in beaten egg yolks and cook 1 minute longer. Stir in butter and vanilla; set aside to cool slightly.

To assemble: For an attractive presentation, use a straight-sided glass bowl or pedestal that will allow the ladyfingers to stand straight up around the outside edges. A 2-quart soufflé dish also works well.

Cut pound cake into slices about 1–1½ inches thick, then cut slices into large pieces to fit the bottom of the bowl. Without breaking the ladyfingers apart, separate the 2 sections and arrange the ladyfingers, with the rounded side facing outward, in a circle in the bowl, so the tops of the ladyfingers are about 2 inches above the rim of the bowl. (You may need to build up cake layer on the bottom, depending on height of your bowl.)

Sprinkle cake lightly with cream sherry. Spoon sauce over cake and sprinkle with almonds. Top with ⅓ of custard. Repeat layers, ending with custard. Sprinkle lightly with any remaining almonds; garnish with mounds of whipped cream.

If you use freshly whipped cream or a solid whipped topping, you can decorate the top ahead of time. However, if you use a spray can type of whipped cream, do it at the last minute before serving, since it does not have staying power and will melt after a short time.

SERVES 12

ZUCCHINI CAKE

When I taught at the College of the Canyons in California, one of my students developed this recipe.

1 cup raisins
1 cup Madeira wine
2 eggs
⅔ cup vegetable oil
1 cup firmly packed brown sugar
1 cup whole wheat flour
1½ teaspoons soda
2 teaspoons ground cinnamon
½ teaspoon salt
2 cups grated zucchini
1 teaspoon minced fresh ginger
1 cup chopped walnuts
**Additional cinnamon and nuts for bottom
of Bundt dish**

On the day before, place raisins in small bowl, and cover with wine to soak overnight.

In bowl, beat eggs until just blended. Add oil and sugar; beat until thoroughly mixed. Stir together flour, soda, cinnamon, and salt. Stir into egg mixture. Add zucchini, ginger, well-drained raisins, and nuts.

Sprinkle bottom and sides of a 6-cup Bundt or ring mold with cinnamon and finely chopped nuts. Pour mixture evenly into dish. (Drink wine!)

Cook on high (600–700 watts) for 11–12 minutes, just until bread begins to pull slightly away from the sides. (The top will still be moist.) Use a toothpick or wood skewer to test. Turn only if it appears to be cooking unevenly.

Allow to cool on flat surface. Turn out on attractive round serving dish. You may sprinkle with powdered sugar, but it can stand on its own just as it is.

SERVES 8

GINGERBREAD RING

This cake makes the house smell like Grandmother is in the kitchen—cooking! Works best in a ring mold.

2¼ cups flour
2 teaspoons freshly grated gingerroot *or* 1
    teaspoon ground ginger
1½ teaspoons baking soda
1 teaspoon ground cinnamon
½ teaspoon salt
⅛ teaspoon ground cloves
½ cup butter (1 stick), softened
½ cup packed brown sugar
½ cup granulated sugar
2 eggs
1 cup buttermilk
1 cup molasses
2 tablespoons grated orange rind
½ teaspoon ground cinnamon
2 teaspoons brown sugar

Mix first 6 ingredients together in a bowl and set aside. Cream together butter and sugars. Add eggs, buttermilk, molasses, and orange rind. Stir in flour mixture and blend.

Sprinkle a 10-cup Bundt pan with cinnamon and brown sugar. Pour mixture into pan.

Cook on medium high (400–500 watts) for 13–15 minutes, turning if gingerbread appears to be cooking unevenly. Allow to cool on a heatproof flat surface 10 minutes before unmolding onto a serving plate.

SERVES 10–12

PUMPKIN CAKE

If you have fresh pumpkins around the house for Hallow-een, why not recycle your jack-o'-lanterns? Pumpkin is a member of the squash family and may be cooked whole or in pieces. The rind may be left on or taken off. It will cook faster with the outer shell off, but I find it easier simply to wash it and cook it in nature's own package. Pierce the outer shell, unless it has a face cut out, and cook it on high (600–700 watts) about 7 minutes per pound or until fork tender.

1 cup sugar
1 cup fresh or canned mashed cooked
    pumpkin
⅓ cup vegetable oil
½ cup buttermilk
2 eggs
½ cup golden raisins
¼ cup chopped dried apricots
1⅔ cups flour
1 teaspoon baking soda
½ teaspoon salt
3 rounded teaspoons pumpkin pie spice
1 cup chopped walnuts, divided

Blend first 5 ingredients in mixing bowl. Add all remaining ingredients but a little pumpkin pie spice and ¼ cup of chopped nuts. Beat at medium speed until just blended. Sprinkle ¼ cup nuts into a 6-cup ring mold, along with a sprinkling of pumpkin pie spice.

Fill mold with mixture. If you have a rack, elevate the mold. Cook on medium high (400–500 watts) for 13–15 minutes, turning if it appears to be cooking unevenly. Allow to cool on a heatproof flat surface before unmolding.

SERVES 6–8

CARROT CAKE

Moist and colorful with a taste to match. Moist fillings like shredded carrots, combined with oil, work well in the micro- wave. Like most cakes of this size, the center does not cook, because the density and moisture require all the microwave energy from the outside in, leaving little cooking action for the inside area. Therefore, we use special microwave baking tech- niques and a microwave ring mold (or Bundt pan). With the center removed, the results are excellent.

> **2 cups flour**
> **2 teaspoons ground cinnamon**
> **1½ teaspoons baking soda**
> **1 teaspoon ground nutmeg**
> **½ teaspoon salt**
> **3 cups grated carrots**
> **1 8-ounce can crushed pineapple, well drained**
> **1 cup shredded coconut**
> **1½ cups sugar**
> **1 cup vegetable oil**
> **1 cup chopped walnuts**
> **3 eggs, well beaten**
> **Buttermilk Glaze (optional) (see recipe below) *or* Cream Cheese Frosting (see index)**

Combine first 5 ingredients and set aside. Combine carrots, pineapple, coconut, sugar, oil, and nuts and blend well. Stir in eggs. Add dry ingredients and mix thoroughly. Turn into 12-inch microwave Bundt pan.

Cook on high (600–700 watts) for 11–14 minutes, turning pan if cake appears to be cooking unevenly. When done, cake will pull slightly away from pan. Cool before inverting onto serving plate. To make it easier for cake to fall out of the pan, use a sharp knife to loosen cake around edges and around the center post. If you like frosting, you may use the Buttermilk Glaze or Cream Cheese Frosting.

SERVES 10–12

BUTTERMILK GLAZE

¾ cup sugar
½ teaspoon baking soda
½ cup buttermilk
¼ pound (1 stick) butter
1 tablespoon light corn syrup
2 teaspoons vanilla

Combine all ingredients but vanilla in a 1-quart glass measure. Cook on high (600–700 watts) for 2 minutes. Stir well and continue to cook on high for 4–5 minutes, until slightly thickened, stirring once. Stir in vanilla.

MAKES ABOUT 2 CUPS

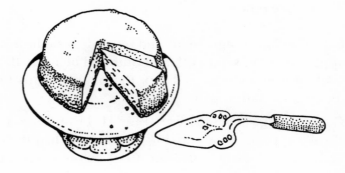

CARAMELIZED RAISIN-NUT RING

*If you keep refrigerated buttermilk biscuits in your refriger-
ator, this can be a handy recipe in a pinch, when unexpected
guests drop in for coffee and you can't find a thing to serve.*

> **3 tablespoons butter or margarine**
> **⅓ cup brown sugar**
> **2 tablespoons light corn syrup**
> **½ cup chopped nuts**
> **¼ cup raisins**
> **½ teaspoon cinnamon**
> **1 10-ounce roll refrigerated buttermilk
> biscuits**

Melt butter in 6-cup ring mold. Stir in sugar and corn
syrup. Spread in mold. Sprinkle nuts, raisins, and cinnamon
evenly. Cook on high (600–700 watts) for 1 minute to set. Place
biscuits around the mold over sugar mixture. Bake on medium
(300–350 watts) for 7–10 minutes or until biscuits are no longer
doughy. If ring appears to be rising unevenly, rotate dish. To
unmold, invert on serving dish.

SERVES 8–10

PIE SHELLS

Crumb Crusts
Sweet Pie Crust
Basic Pie Crust

PIES AND TARTS

Apple Pie
Pecan Pie
Banana Cream Pie
Coconut Nectarine Cream Pie
Fresh Strawberry Pie
Perfect Lemon Meringue Pie
Fresh Peach Pie
Hawaiian Crunch Pie
Fresh Fruit Tart with Orange Glaze
Grasshopper Pie

2
PIES

The greatest advantage to preparing your own pies is the ability to control the amount of sugar. By using fresh fruits in season, you can produce the sweetest of pies that are certain to become family favorites. If fresh fruits are not available, there are a variety of frozen fruits of excellent quality (some with no sugar), because they are fast-frozen at the peak of their maturity. Keeping a supply in your freezer, as well as frozen or refrigerated unbaked pie shells, means you do not need to visit your bakery to produce a lovely pie at whim.

Remember that in microwave cooking the pie shell must always be completely cooked before it is filled. Otherwise, the shell will not cook. Once the pie shell is filled with ingredients, the microwave energy prefers the pie filling, which it reaches first, and will concentrate there, without really becoming involved with the bottom layer, which remains uncooked.

For most of my pies, I prefer to precook the shell and cook the pie filling in the microwave separately, then simply combine them for an outstanding presentation and taste. It is simple, fast, and tastes as though it had been in an oven for an hour.

Pie Shells

There are many ways to enjoy a homemade pie in the microwave. Experiment with the suggestions for tasty microwave pie crusts that follow to determine which flavorings and other additions you prefer.

CRUMB CRUSTS

Crumb crusts are easy to make in minutes and give good flavor to a homemade custard or fruit filling that is cooked first, then combined with the crust and refrigerated until served.

You can use your favorite cookie, blended into crumbs in a food processor or blender, combined with some melted butter or margarine and baked for 1-2 minutes or simply refrigerated until firm.

To keep a ready supply, place all leftover crumbs from the cookie jar or from cakes and pastries in a refrigerated jar. If they include some crumbled raisins and nuts, all the better. Use this mixture instead of graham crackers for a rich crust for a fruit or custard pie. Just melt a tablespoon or two of butter or margarine in a 9" pie plate, stir in 1½ cups of leftover crumbled sweets, and pat into bottom and sides of plate. Cook on high (600–700 watts) for 30 seconds and chill until ready to use.

Nuts and coconut also can be used to give a special flavor that will complement the pie fillings. They also look good when slightly cooked in the microwave before filling.

Cookies like macaroons make an interesting variation. These are just a few suggestions; use your imagination and combine cookies to delight your family and guests.

> 5 tablespoons butter or margarine
> 1¼ cups fine crumbs (vanilla wafers, graham crackers, ginger snaps, chocolate wafers, cream sandwich cookies, etc.)
> 1 tablespoon sugar

In a 9″ pie plate or quiche dish, melt butter on high (600–700 watts) 1 minute. Blend in crumbs and sugar. If desired, set aside 2 tablespoons crumb mixture to sprinkle on top of pie. Press crumb mixture firmly and evenly over bottom and sides of plate. Cook on high 1½ minutes. Cool before filling.

MAKES ONE 9″ PIE SHELL

SWEET PIE CRUST

This is good for fruit pies, such as the Fresh Fruit Tart with Orange Glaze (see index). It is easy to prepare with a food processor. It is a soft dough, easy to roll and shape.

1¼ cups flour
½ cup cake flour
2 tablespoons sugar
½ teaspoon salt
⅔ cup butter-flavored vegetable shortening
¼–⅓ cup ice-cold milk
Egg wash (1 beaten egg)

Combine all ingredients but milk and egg wash in food processor container with metal blade. Process with short pulses until shortening disappears. Add milk slowly through the feed tube and continue to process with short pulses just until it begins to come together, but before it forms a ball. Gather dough together and form a ball. Wrap in plastic and refrigerate about 1 hour.

Roll between two pieces of plastic wrap. Place in 9″ pie plate or quiche dish. With a pastry brush, brush entire crust with egg wash. Pierce all over with prongs of a fork.

Cook on high (600–700 watts) 6–7 minutes, until crust becomes crisp and a few brown spots appear. Set aside to cool before filling.

MAKES ONE 9″ PIE SHELL

BASIC PIE CRUST

Because we do not have a hot dry environment in the microwave, we do not produce the same type of brown crust. However, this recipe is crisp and delicious and can be made attractive by using microwave techniques.

Baking time will vary, depending on the thickness of the dough and the amount of glaze used on top. The dough is done when it is no longer doughy and feels crisp to the touch. I always wait for a brown spot to appear as a signal that the pie shell is done.

This is simple to prepare in your food processor or by hand. It is easy to work and to roll out and is flaky when baked in the microwave. Here are the directions for the food processor.

> **2 cups flour**
> **¼ teaspoon salt**
> **¼ pound (½ cup) vegetable shortening, chilled**
> **⅓-½ cup ice-cold water**

Place flour and salt in the food processor bowl, using metal blade. Cut shortening into pieces and place in circle on top of flour. Process with half-second pulses until shortening disappears. Add water and process with half-second pulses just until water is absorbed and dough begins to come together. Stop before it forms a ball.

Remove dough and press together into a ball. Wrap in plastic and refrigerate for about 1 hour before rolling dough out. It can be frozen at this point.

To bake, roll out dough into two pie shells. Press into a 9″ pie plate. Trim crusts ¼ inch beyond pie plate rim (it will shrink slightly as it bakes). Apply a beaten egg wash with a pastry brush to seal and glaze crust. (See variations on following page.) Cook on high 6–8 minutes. (See variations below for sealing suggestions.) Always pierce pie crust with a fork on bottom and sides of pastry before baking to prevent the crust from puffing up during baking.

MAKES TWO 9″ PIE SHELLS

VARIATIONS

The following can be added to the flour for flavoring and color:

- *Spices*—1 tablespoon sugar, 1 teaspoon cinnamon, ⅛ teaspoon cloves, or ⅛ teaspoon nutmeg for each 9″ pie crust
- *Nuts*—¼ cup chopped nuts, plus cinnamon, nutmeg, and cloves
- *Chocolate*—2 tablespoons unsweetened cocoa powder, plus 2 tablespoons sugar

The following can be added to the liquid that is added to the pie crust dough as it is mixed:

- *Food coloring*—2 drops yellow food coloring
- *Vanilla*—1 teaspoon vanilla
- *Coffee*—1 tablespoon coffee (liquid)
- *Cocoa*—1 tablespoon cocoa (liquid)

To produce a good seal, plus a nice glaze, brush the entire pastry shell after it is placed in the pie plate with any of the following:

- 1 beaten egg
- 1 egg yolk mixed with 1 teaspoon water
- 1 teaspoon vanilla mixed with ½ teaspoon water

APPLE PIE

Most fruit pies can be prepared by using this microwave cooking technique: prebaking the pie shell, then cooking the filling until just the right texture, and finally combining the two. I like to do all types of fresh fruit pies this way. You won't believe how simple it is to enjoy summer fruits in this manner. If you do not care to make your own pie shell, buy the refrigerated pie shells, just waiting to be placed in your pie plate, coated with a beaten egg, and baked for about 6-7 minutes.

1 prebaked 9″ pie shell
(see index for pie crust recipes)
7 large tart cooking apples
Grated rind of 1 small lemon
Juice of 1 small lemon
½ cup brown sugar
3 tablespoons flour
1 teaspoon ground cinnamon
½ teaspoon freshly grated nutmeg
2 tablespoons dark corn syrup
1 teaspoon vanilla
¼ cup butter
Whipped cream for garnish

Set aside pie shell to cool. Pare, core, and slice apples. Place in 2-quart bowl. Remove rind from lemon. Squeeze lemon juice over apples as you slice them and place them in the bowl to prevent discoloring. In another bowl, combine sugar, flour, cinnamon, and nutmeg. Sprinkle dry mixture over each layer of apples as you add them to bowl. Sprinkle with corn syrup, vanilla, lemon rind and dot with butter. Cover with Bounty

Microwave paper towel. Cook on high (600–700 watts) 15–17 minutes, stirring frequently but gently with a wooden spoon. When apples begin to caramelize, spoon into cooled pie shell.

To serve, decorate with whipped cream and serve remaining whipped cream on side.

SERVES 6–8

PECAN PIE

Definitely not for dieters, but worth every calorie. Great with vanilla ice cream or a touch of whipped cream.

¼ cup (½ stick) **unsalted butter**
2 cups **whole pecans**
1 cup **sugar**
1 cup **light or dark corn syrup**
3 eggs, **lightly beaten**
1 teaspoon **vanilla**
1 prebaked 9″ **pie shell (see index for pie crust recipes)**

Melt butter in 2-quart measure on high (600–700 watts). Add nuts, sugar, corn syrup, eggs, and vanilla and blend well. Pour into pie shell. Cook on medium high (400–500 watts) until center is set, about 11–12 minutes. Turn pie if it appears to be cooking unevenly.

Serve either at room temperature or chilled.

SERVES 6

BANANA CREAM PIE

If bananas are not one of your favorites, make it anyway and substitute your favorite fruit—or just serve it as a not-too-sweet, creamy custard pie. The sugar has been cut to a minimum for better taste.

It is so simple to prepare a silky custard in your microwave with cornstarch, milk, and egg yolks that there is no need ever to use an overly sweet prepared mix.

Remember, if you eat a banana each day, you are filling your body's need for potassium!

CRUST

⅓ cup butter

1½ cups vanilla wafer crumbs
   (approximately 35 cookies)

¼ cup sugar

FILLING

⅔ cup sugar

⅓ cup cornstarch

½ teaspoon salt

2½ cups milk

4 egg yolks

2 tablespoons butter

2 teaspoons vanilla

½ teaspoon banana extract (optional)

3 large firm bananas

Sweetened whipped cream (optional, but a
   nice touch)

For crust: Place butter in a 9″ pie plate. Melt on high (600–700 watts) for ¾–1 minute. Stir crumbs and sugar together until well combined, then press into the pie plate to form a pie shell. Refrigerate until set. (Cooking this crust will make it too hard—and there is no need.)

For filling: Combine sugar, cornstarch, and salt in 2-quart glass measure or bowl. Add milk a bit at a time, stirring until cornstarch is completely dissolved. Add egg yolks, using a whisk to combine well. Cook on high for 6–7½ minutes, stirring once or twice, until mixture comes to a boil. Stir in the butter and vanilla (and banana extract if using). Allow to cool slightly. (If you layer the custard and bananas in the shell while the custard is still hot, the layers tend to separate.)

After the custard has cooled to room temperature, peel and slice 2 bananas about ⅛–¼ inch thick. Arrange half the slices in the pie shell. Cover with half the custard. Place a second layer of sliced bananas over custard and top with remaining custard. Chill thoroughly.

Just before serving, slice remaining banana and arrange over top. If desired, spoon whipped cream over top of pie or over each individual slice when serving.

SERVES 6

COCONUT NECTARINE CREAM PIE

If fresh nectarines are out of season, any fresh fruit may be substituted. Use ripe fruit that yields slightly to palm pressure. This coconut cream pie is a wonderful combination of chewy coconut and smooth cream, ringed with wedges of fresh fruit. Serve pie and fuit at room temperature for optimum flavor.

1 prebaked 9" Basic Pie Crust (see index)
½ cup sugar
2 tablespoons cornstarch
1½ cups milk
2 egg yolks
½ teaspoon vanilla
½ cup dairy sour cream
3 fresh nectarines, peaches, or other fruit
    cut into wedges
½ cup toasted shredded coconut, divided
2 tablespoons butter

Let baked pie shell cool

Combine sugar, cornstarch, and a small amount of the milk in 1-quart bowl. Stir until cornstarch is completely dissolved. Add remaining milk. Cook on high (600–700 watts) about 3 minutes, until mixture comes to a boil, stirring once. Stir. Continue to cook on high 1 minute.

Beat egg yolks in small bowl. Beat in some of the hot mixture, then pour egg yolks into milk mixture. Mix well and cook on high 1 minute. Blend in vanilla and set aside to cool for 15 minutes.

Melt butter in glass measure on high for 1 minute. Stir in coconut to absorb melted butter. Cook on high for 2 minutes, or until brown spots begin to appear.

Beat in sour cream and fold ¼ cup toasted coconut into filling, and turn into shell. Place nectarine wedges around edges of baked pie shell, points radiating out like petals. Sprinkle with remaining ¼ cup coconut. Chill 1 hour until set.

SERVES 6–8

FRESH STRAWBERRY PIE

A lovely pie with a delicate clear glaze. Not too sweet.

1 prebaked 9″ Basic Pie Crust (see index)
5 cups fresh strawberries
1 cup water
3 tablespoons cornstarch
3 tablespoons water
½ cup sugar
Red food coloring
Whipped cream (optional)

Cool baked pie shell.

Pick through the strawberries and place 1 cup of the smaller, less attractive ones in a 4-cup glass measure. Add 1 cup water. Cook on high (600–700 watts) 4 minutes, stirring once. Pour through a sieve and return sieved liquid to the 4-cup glass measure.

Combine cornstarch with 3 tablespoons water, stir until cornstarch is dissolved. Stir cornstarch mixture and sugar into strawberry juice. Continue to cook on high 2 minutes, just until mixture begins to thicken and clear, stirring once. Add several drops of food coloring.

Arrange whole berries in pie shell with larger ones in the center. Pour glaze over berries and chill.

SERVES 6

PERFECT LEMON MERINGUE PIE

Custard, at its best, is a mouth-watering, fresh-tasting dessert. You can't miss when you combine fresh eggs with fresh lemon juice to create this delectably tart lemon pie. Make the most of your microwave by heating the lemons on high (600–700 watts) for about 50 seconds to get maximum juice out of them. (See photo.)

> 1 prebaked Basic Pie Crust (see index)
> 1¼ cups sugar
> ⅓ cup cornstarch
> 1½ cups water
> ¼ teaspoon salt
> 6 extra-large eggs, separated
> 3 tablespoons butter
> ½ cup lemon juice (2 large lemons)
> 3 tablespoons grated lemon rind, divided
> ½ cup sugar
> ¼ teaspoon cream of tartar
> ½ teaspoon vanilla

After baking pie shell, set aside to cool.

Combine 1¼ cups sugar and the cornstarch in a 2-quart glass measure or bowl. Stir in water gradually and continue stirring until cornstarch is completely dissolved. Add salt. Cook on high (600–700 watts), stirring every 2 minutes, until thick and clear, about 6–8 minutes.

Beat egg yolks until thick and creamy. Pour a little of the cooked mixture into the yolks, blend well, then add all the yolks to mixture. Cook on high 2 minutes. Blend in butter, lemon juice, and ½ the lemon rind. Blend. Pour into cooled pie shell.

In large mixing bowl, beat egg whites until foamy. Combine ½ cup sugar and the cream of tartar and gradually add to whites, continuing to beat until glossy and soft peaks form. Beat in vanilla.

With a rubber spatula, spread meringue completely over top of pie so that no filling shows, making certain the meringue seals the crust all around. Sprinkle top with remaining lemon rind.

To set meringue, place in microwave and cook on high 2 minutes. This will set meringue but not brown it. If you prefer a traditional browned meringue, place pie under preheated broiler for about 2 minutes, until lightly browned. Cool before serving. Lemon pie tastes best at room temperature.

SERVES 6-8

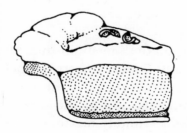

FRESH PEACH PIE

I found this in Dinah Shore's first cookbook, Someone's in the Kitchen with Dinah, *and she says she had to repeat it in her second book. She calls it summer madness; it must be made with fresh peaches. I do the crust in the microwave. The flavors interact with the peach and sour cream mixture, and the first time I tried it, it served only two—me and my husband Mo!*

COCONUT ALMOND CRUST

1 cup blanched almonds
1 cup canned moist-style flaked coconut
¼ cup sugar
¼ cup butter or margarine

FILLING

1 cup sour cream
6 tablespoons confectioners' (powdered) sugar, divided
1 teaspoon orange juice
1 teaspoon shredded orange rind
1 teaspoon vanilla
3 cups peeled and sliced fresh peaches
1 cup whipping cream

For crust: Grind almonds medium-fine. Mix with coconut. Work in sugar and butter with fingers or spoon. Press evenly into bottom and sides of a 9″ pie plate, fluting edges to make an attractive rim reaching the top of the sides of the pie plate, reserving 3 tablespoons crumbly mixture for the top. Cook on high (600–700 watts) for 6–9 minutes, watching carefully that it does not burn in spots. Let stand until completely cool; it will firm as it cools.

Place remaining crumb mixture, spreading well, in a shallow dish and toast in microwave on high for a few minutes. Set aside.

For filling: Beat sour cream with 4 tablespoons powdered sugar, orange juice, orange rind, and vanilla. Spread on bottom and sides of cooled shell. (The filling will be thin, but it will thicken as it stands.) Cover with peaches arranged in a sunburst pattern, with slices overlapping.

Whip cream and fold in remaining 2 tablespoons powdered sugar. Cover peaches with whipped cream. Sprinkle top with reserved toasted coconut mixture. Chill until ready to serve.

SERVES 6

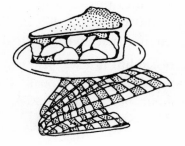

HAWAIIAN CRUNCH PIE

Rich, rich, sensuous pie. Don't worry if you have to work it off later—it's worth it!

It goes well with a Crumb Crust made with macaroons—a nut crust, or a simple pie shell.

> 1 prebaked 9″ pie shell made from Basic
> Pie Crust, Nut Crust, or Crumb Crust
> using macaroons (see index)
> ¾ cup sugar, divided
> 1 envelope unflavored gelatin
> 2 teaspoons instant coffee powder
> 2 tablespoons unsweetened cocoa powder
> 2 tablespoons Kahlua
> ½ teaspoon salt
> 1½ cups milk
> 2 egg yolks, beaten
> 2 egg whites
> ¼ teaspoon cream of tartar
> 1 cup whipping cream, divided
> ¼ cup chopped almonds
> Chocolate Leaves (optional) (see index)

In a 1-quart glass measure, combine ½ cup of the sugar, the gelatin, instant coffee powder, cocoa, Kahlua, and salt. Stir in milk. Let stand 5 minutes to soften gelatin. Stir in egg yolks. Cook on high (600–700 watts) for 4–5 minutes, until mixture thickens slightly, stirring twice with a whisk. Cool completely.

When it has cooled but not set, beat egg whites with cream of tartar in a small bowl until soft peaks form. Gradually add remaining ¼ cup sugar, beating until stiff. Fold into thickened gelatin mixture.

Whip ½ cup cream until stiff. Refrigerate remaining ½ cup. Fold whipped cream carefully into gelatin mixture. Pour into prebaked pie crust. Chill several hours or overnight. May also be frozen.

Before serving pie, whip remaining cream. Spoon or pipe whipped cream around edge. Garnish with chopped nuts and Chocolate Leaves, if desired.

SERVES 8

FRESH FRUIT TART WITH ORANGE GLAZE

There are few desserts as attractive and satisfying as a tart, combining a bit of sweetness in the crust, a layer of either cream cheese or custard, and seasonal fruit attractively arranged over the prebaked shell and glazed with a fresh fruit liquid glaze. Using a minimum amount of sugar is possible, since nature's sweetness is in your fruit. (See photo.)

Use whatever fruit you like, of one kind or several in combination. You can also purchase prebaked individual tart shells in many food shops. These are excellent in quality and will save you some time.

1 9″ prebaked pie shell made from Sweet
    Pie Crust (see index)
3 3-ounce packages cream cheese, softened
    in microwave for 30 seconds
½ cup confectioners' (powdered) sugar
3–4 cups fruit, such as sliced peaches,
    bananas, apricots, grapes, whole or
    sliced strawberries, blueberries,
    raspberries, fresh sliced pineapple

ORANGE GLAZE

1 tablespoon plus 1 teaspoon cornstarch
1 cup orange juice
¼ cup sugar
2 teaspoons grated orange rind
1 tablespoon orange-flavored liqueur
    (optional)

For tart: Set aside pie shell to cool.

With an electric mixer, whip cream cheese and powdered sugar together until light and fluffy. Spread in bottom of cooled prebaked pie shell. Arrange fruit as desired.

For glaze: Mix cornstarch with orange juice until dissolved in 1-quart glass measure. Add remaining ingredients. Cook on high (600–700 watts) 2–3 minutes, stirring twice, until mixture begins to thicken.

Spoon Orange Glaze over fruit, covering fruit completely. May be refrigerated up to 8 hours.

SERVES 5–6

GRASSHOPPER PIE

The use of marshmallows to produce a creamy, luscious pie is a perfect microwave technique. It can become the base with the addition of liquid for almost any pie of your choice— chocolate, lemon, and a beautiful holiday favorite, the Grasshopper.

Served at a Christmas buffet, it is a festive touch of green with a refreshing crème de menthe flavor that people enjoy after an evening of feasting.

1½ cups chocolate wafer crumbs
¼ cup (½ stick) melted butter
4 cups miniature marshmallows
½ cup milk
¼ cup white crème de cacao
¼ cup green crème de menthe
2 cups whipping cream, whipped
Chocolate Curls for garnish (see index)

Combine crumbs and butter in a 9″ pie plate. (You can melt the butter first, right in the pie plate.) Press into bottom and up the sides of 9″ pie plate. Refrigerate until ready to use.

Combine marshmallows and milk in 2-quart bowl. Cook on high (600–700 watts) until marshmallows begin to melt, about 2–2½ minutes. Stir until completely melted. Let cool slightly. Blend in liqueurs. Let cool until the bottom of the bowl is completely cool. (It's best to do this at room temperature to keep the marshmallows soft enough to mix in the whipped cream.)

Fold in all but ½ cup whipped cream. Spoon into prepared crust. Garnish with remaining whipped cream. Sprinkle with Chocolate Curls. Refrigerate until firm.

SERVES 6–8

Chocolate Pudding
Pudding Parfait
Chocolate Almond Pudding
Floating Islands
Maple Nut Pudding
Fluffy Tapioca Pudding
Old-Fashioned Bread Pudding
Indian Pudding
Fresh Apple Mousse with Apricot Sauce
Velvet Mousse with Chocolate Curls
Kahlua Chocolate Almond Mousse
A White or Chocolate Mousse
Lemon Pineapple Creme
Creme Caramel

3
PUDDINGS AND MOUSSES

It is so simple to cook a pudding in the microwave, and the flavor so superior—not to mention the reduced amount of sugar—that this technique may become a favorite. If there are children in the home, teach them to do it for themselves.

A mousse is a cloud of texture that for many people is the perfect dessert. A pure microwave technique substitutes marshmallows for the egg whites to give the mousse its heavenly texture.

CHOCOLATE PUDDING

Even if you purchase store-bought pudding, do try one in your microwave. Think how nice it will be not to have scorched bottoms on your pots!

I have cut the sugar down. If you prefer it sweeter, increase the sugar to ⅔ cup.

> ½ **cup sugar**
> ¼ **cup unsweetened cocoa powder**
> 3 **tablespoons cornstarch**
> 2¼ **cups whole or low-fat milk**
> 2 **tablespoons butter**
> 1 **teaspoon vanilla**

Combine sugar, cocoa, and cornstarch in 8-cup glass measure. Gradually stir in a little milk and stir until cornstarch is completely dissolved. Add remaining milk.

Cook on high (600–700 watts) for 7–10 minutes, stirring every 2 minutes. Cooking is finished when mixture is cooked through and begins to thicken. Stir in butter and vanilla. Pour into individual serving dishes. Cover with plastic wrap pressed down on pudding surface to prevent skin from forming over top. Refrigerate until chilled and serve.

SERVES 4

PUDDING PARFAIT

Create a luscious parfait by combining two puddings in a parfait glass.

> **Chocolate Almond Pudding (see index)**
> **Maple Nut Pudding (see index)**
> **Whipped cream**
> **Chopped nuts (any type) for garnish**

Make sure you use 2 parts Chocolate Almond Pudding to 1 part Maple Nut Pudding or vice versa.

Divide 4 parfait glasses into thirds and spoon Chocolate Almond Pudding into the bottom third of each. Top with a layer of Maple Nut Pudding and fill the top third with the Chocolate Almond Pudding. Add a generous dollop of whipped cream and sprinkle with additional nuts of your choice.

SERVES 4

CHOCOLATE ALMOND PUDDING

3 tablespoons cornstarch
2 cups milk, divided
⅓ cup sugar
1 cup chocolate chips
1 tablespoon butter
2 egg yolks, beaten
1 teaspoon vanilla
½ cup sliced or slivered almonds
Whipped cream (optional)

In a 2-quart glass measure, blend cornstarch with 1 cup milk. Stir until cornstarch is completely dissolved. Add remaining milk, the sugar, and the chocolate chips and stir to blend. Cook on high (600–700 watts) 6 minutes, stirring after 4 minutes. Mix in butter. Add some of the hot mixture to the beaten egg yolks and mix well. Whisk egg mixture into milk and continue to cook on high 30 seconds.

Stir in vanilla and almonds, reserving a few almonds to sprinkle over top. Refrigerate to cool before serving. Whipped cream on top is a welcome addition; just save the almonds to place on the whipped cream instead of the pudding.

SERVES 4

FLOATING ISLANDS

A popular microwave dessert, using the soft meringue technique, that is fun to cook. A good children's recipe, but I make it even when I don't expect my grandchildren to stop by.

½ cup sugar
3 tablespoons cornstarch
2¾ cups milk, divided
1 teaspoon vanilla
2 egg yolks, well beaten
2 egg whites
⅛ teaspoon cream of tartar
¼ cup sugar
¼ cup almonds
1 teaspoon butter

In a 2-quart glass measure, blend sugar and cornstarch. Add ¾ cup milk and whisk until cornstarch is completely dissolved. Add remaining milk. Cook on high (600–700 watts) for 4 minutes. Mix well and continue to cook about 4 more minutes, just until mixture thickens. Mix in vanilla.

Stir a small amount of hot pudding quickly into beaten egg yolks. Whisking constantly, return egg mixture to hot pudding, mixing well. Continue to cook 30 seconds. Pour into serving bowl and set aside to cool. (Use a shallow bowl, wide enough on top to hold meringue puffs.)

When pudding has cooled, beat egg whites until foamy. Add cream of tartar. Gradually add sugar, beating until whites are stiff.

Drop the meringue in 8–10 mounds on a sheet of waxed paper in a circle. Cook on medium (300–350 watts) for 1½–2 minutes or until set. Allow to cool slightly. Slide meringues on top of cooled pudding.

Place almonds and butter in a 1-cup glass measure. Cook on high (600–700 watts) 1–3 minutes, stirring twice, just until almonds become hot and slightly crisp.

Sprinkle over Islands and serve immediately or refrigerate until ready to serve.

SERVES 4–6

MAPLE NUT PUDDING

½ **cup firmly packed brown sugar**
3 **tablespoons cornstarch**
2 **cups milk, divided**
4 **egg yolks**
1 **tablespoon butter**
2 **tablespoons maple syrup**
1 **teaspoon vanilla**
½ **cup chopped walnuts or pecans**
Whipped cream (optional)

Combine sugar, cornstarch, and 1 cup of milk in a 2-quart glass measure. Stir until cornstarch is completely dissolved. Stir in remaining milk. Cook on high (600–700 watts) 6 minutes, stirring after 3–4 minutes.

Beat egg yolks in small bowl and add ½ cup of hot milk mixture, using whisk to blend quickly. Whisk egg mixture back into milk. Continue to cook on high 30 seconds, just until mixture is thickened. Stir in butter, maple syrup, vanilla, and nuts, reserving a few nuts to sprinkle on top. Refrigerate to cool before serving.

If you use a dollop of whipped cream before serving, reserve the nuts to sprinkle on the whipped cream.

SERVES 4

FLUFFY
TAPIOCA PUDDING

I always included this recipe in my basic microwave cooking workshop but never wrote up the recipe for my students. I would read it off the box and show how to adapt it to microwave—no double boilers, no constant stirring and, if you get busy, not to worry: the timer shuts the cooking off automatically.

There were groans from some of the students whenever tapioca was mentioned. I couldn't understand this because I adore this method of preparing it, and when I use low-fat milk and cut the sugar, I have a luscious low-calorie dessert to enjoy without guilt. I still had the negative response. I finally discovered that my students' aversion to tapioca began with the lumpy, dried-out version many of them had been served, usually at summer camp. With a great deal of persistence, I was able to convince them to try one small taste, and the conversion rate was 100 percent!

In following the package recipe, I increased the amount of vanilla to compensate for the sweetness lost when I reduced the amount of sugar.

> 3 rounded tablespoons minute tapioca
> 4 tablespoons sugar, divided
> 1 egg yolk
> ⅛ teaspoon salt
> 2 cups milk (whole or low-fat)
> 1 teaspoon vanilla
> 1 egg white
> Freshly grated nutmeg
> Whipped cream (optional)

In a 4-cup glass measure, combine tapioca, 2 tablespoons of the sugar, the egg yolk, salt, and milk. Let stand 5 minutes to soften the tapioca. Use a wire whisk to whisk egg yolk briskly into the milk. Cook on high (600–700 watts) 6–7 minutes, whisking once or twice, until mixture begins to thicken. Timing will depend on the starting temperature of the milk. Stir in vanilla.

When thickened like pudding, set aside (it will thicken as it cools) and beat egg white until foamy. Gradually beat in 2 tablespoons of sugar, beating to soft peaks. Fold the beaten egg white into the warm pudding, just until blended (do not deflate the egg whites).

Pour into attractive serving dish or 4 individual serving dishes. Sprinkle with nutmeg. Serve with dollops of whipped cream, if desired. May be served warm or chilled.

SERVES 4

TAPIOCA PUDDING VARIATIONS

Tapioca and Fruit Parfaits: Spoon ¼ cup apricot, blueberry, cherry, peach, or strawberry pie filling into each of 4 sherbet dishes or parfait glasses. Top each with ½ cup tapioca and garnish with a spoonful of pie filling.

OLD-FASHIONED BREAD PUDDING

This works best in a ring mold. Although it has been updated for the microwave, it has that old-fashioned flavor.

> 1 3-ounce package cream cheese
> 2 cups milk
> 2 teaspoons vanilla
> ½ cup chopped walnuts
> ½ cup golden raisins
> 6 slices French bread, cut ½ inch thick, toasted and broken into pieces
> ¼ cup butter
> 1 cup brown sugar
> 1 teaspoon ground nutmeg
> 1 teaspoon ground cinnamon
> ¼ teaspoon salt
> 3 eggs, well beaten
> Confectioners' (powdered) sugar (optional)

In a 4-cup glass measure, combine cream cheese and milk. Heat on high (600–700 watts) 3–4 minutes, stirring twice. Stir in vanilla, walnuts, and raisins. Place bread in a 1-quart ring mold or a round casserole. Pour hot milk mixture over top. Set aside.

Combine butter, brown sugar, nutmeg, cinnamon, and salt in a 4-cup glass measure. Cook on high 1 minute. Stir well. Add eggs and whisk well. Stir into bread mixture and mix gently until combined. Cook on high 6–9 minutes, turning dish if it appears to be cooking unevenly. Sprinkle with powdered sugar if desired.

SERVES 4–6

INDIAN PUDDING

There are many different versions of this pudding, all containing cornmeal, molasses, and similar seasonings. It has a soft texture and is rather thick. The combination of seasonings and molasses makes it a unique and satisfying topping for vanilla ice cream, especially when freshly made whipped cream is added.

2 cups milk
¼ cup yellow cornmeal
2 tablespoons sugar
½ teaspoon salt
½ teaspoon ground cinnamon
¼ teaspoon ground ginger
2 eggs, beaten
¼ cup molasses
1 tablespoon butter
Vanilla ice cream
Whipped cream

Place milk in a 2-quart bowl. Cook on high (600–700 watts) 4 minutes. Meanwhile, combine cornmeal, sugar, salt, cinnamon, and ginger. Stir in hot milk. Continue to cook on medium (300–350 watts) 4 minutes. Meanwhile, blend together eggs and molasses. Stir a small amount of milk mixture into egg mixture. Pour it back into milk mixture, add butter, and stir well. Continue to cook on medium 3 minutes. Let stand 10 minutes before serving warm, topped with vanilla ice cream and whipped cream.

SERVES 4–6

FRESH APPLE MOUSSE WITH APRICOT SAUCE

A light and refreshing dessert that may be made two days ahead.

8 medium apples (any firm cooking apple), peeled, cored, and quartered
1 teaspoon ground cinnamon
⅓ cup apricot preserves
⅛ teaspoon freshly grated nutmeg
¼ teaspoon freshly grated lemon rind
2 teaspoons cornstarch
2¼ cups milk, divided
6 egg yolks
1 cup sugar
2 tablespoons (2 envelopes) unflavored gelatin
¾ cup fresh orange juice
2 teaspoons vanilla
1½ cups heavy cream, whipped

APRICOT SAUCE

1¼ cups apricot preserves
2 tablespoons fresh lemon juice
1 teaspoon grated lemon rind
½ cup apricot or peach brandy
3 tablespoons confectioners' (powdered) sugar
½ cup water

For mousse: Combine apples, cinnamon, apricot preserves, nutmeg, and lemon rind in 2-quart bowl. Cook, covered, on high (600–700 watts) 10–15 minutes, stirring twice, until mixture can easily be mashed with a fork. Press through sieve; reserve the apple puree and discard any liquid. Dissolve cornstarch in ¼ cup milk and set aside.

Place remaining milk in a 4-cup glass measure and heat on high 3–4 minutes, just until heated through. Combine egg yolks and sugar, beat until pale yellow and fluffy. Add beaten yolks and cornstarch mixture to the warmed milk and heat on medium high (400–500 watts) about 5 minutes or until it begins to thicken, stirring twice. Set aside.

Place gelatin and orange juice in glass measure. Let stand 5 minutes, stir, and heat on high 30 seconds. Whisk into hot custard.

Pour custard into large bowl and chill 2 hours, stirring occasionally, until it starts to set. Remove from refrigerator and fold in vanilla, apple puree, and whipped cream. Pour mousse into individual dessert cups or large glass bowl. Chill at least 6 hours or up to 48 hours before serving.

For sauce: Combine all ingredients in a 4-cup measure. Cook on high 7–9 minutes, until preserves are thoroughly dissolved, stirring once. It may be served as is or passed through a fine sieve before chilling.

Serve mousse with Apricot Sauce passed separately.

SERVES 10–12

VELVET MOUSSE
WITH CHOCOLATE CURLS

A cloud of fluff. May be made ahead and frozen. Place in refrigerator a few hours before serving if it is frozen ahead.

¼ cup Kahlua
¼ cup crème de cacao
15 large marshmallows
1 cup whipping cream
Chocolate Curls or Chocolate Leaves for
    garnish (see index)

In a 1-quart glass measure, place Kahlua, crème de cacao, and marshmallows. Cook on high (600–700 watts) 1½–2 minutes, stirring once, until marshmallows are melted. Allow to cool at room temperature rather than in the refrigerator to keep the mixture fluid.

When it is cooled completely (which is important so that you do not deflate the whipped cream), whip the cream until stiff, and slowly pour the marshmallow mixture into whipped cream, continuing to whip. Spoon into serving glasses and chill. Garnish with Chocolate Curls or Chocolate Leaves.

SERVES 4

KAHLUA CHOCOLATE ALMOND MOUSSE

This is what the microwave can do best. I taught this technique in my first class and discovered that one of my former, very enterprising students prepares this as a dessert for several top Los Angeles restaurants. They believe she bakes the mousse in an oven for over an hour.

Use an attractive bowl that just holds the recipe. It does freeze well, and I have often used this recipe as a gift for a dinner host by placing it in an attractive glass that I can leave as a gift. An oversized champagne glass is perfect. (See photo.)

> ¾ **cup milk**
> ¼ **cup Kahlua**
> 1 **8-ounce chocolate almond bar, broken**
> **into pieces**
> 3 **ounces unsweetened baking chocolate,**
> **broken into pieces**
> 4 **heaping cups miniature marshmallows**
> 3 **tablespoons unsweetened cocoa powder**
> 1 **pint whipping cream, whipped,** *or*
> **2 10-ounce cartons solid-whip topping**
> **Chocolate Curls for garnish (see index)**

In a 2-quart bowl, place milk, Kahlua, chocolates, and marshmallows. Cook on high (600–700 watts) for 3–4 minutes, just until marshmallows begin to melt, stirring once. If necessary, use about 30 seconds more to complete melting. (You do not want to heat chocolate too long.)

Stir in the cocoa powder. Set aside until completely cooled. If time permits, cool to room temperature without refrigeration to make it easier to add the whipped cream. If you do place it in the refrigerator, however, allow it to come back to room temperature before adding the cream. When completely cooled, fold in the whipped cream and garnish. Mousse may be made ahead and frozen.

SERVES 6

A WHITE OR
CHOCOLATE MOUSSE

I had a difficult time choosing one of the many versions of the popular chocolate mousse because they are all so very good.

¾ cup sugar

⅓ cup water

4 ounces semisweet or white chocolate

4 egg yolks, beaten

2 tablespoons Cognac or coffee (do not use coffee with white chocolate)

1 cup whipping cream

Combine sugar and water in 1-quart bowl. Cook on high (600–700 watts) until mixture is clear and syrupy, for about 3–4 minutes. Stir in Cognac or coffee and chocolate until melted. (If necessary, heat on high for 30–45 seconds.)

Pour a small amount of chocolate syrup into beaten egg yolks, mix well, and pour egg yolk mixture into syrup mixture. Whisk well. Set aside and allow to cool to room temperature.

When it has completely cooled (if it is still warm, whipped cream will not hold its shape but will melt down), whip the cream until stiff. Fold chocolate mixture thoroughly but lightly into cream, so as not to deflate the cream. Spoon into individual serving dishes or a soufflé dish and chill about 2 hours for the smaller servings and 4 hours for the large dish. Serve cold.

SERVES 4–6

LEMON PINEAPPLE CREME

Refreshing dessert that can be made ahead and refrigerated. An electric mixer plus beaten egg whites make it light and perfect for the ending of a meal.

¾ cup sugar, divided
3 tablespoons cornstarch
1 8-ounce can crushed pineapple, undrained
⅔ cup water
2 eggs, separated
1 teaspoon grated lemon rind
2 tablespoons lemon juice
1 3-ounce package cream cheese, cubed

In 4-cup glass measure, combine ½ cup of the sugar, cornstarch, pineapple and its liquid, and water. Stir until cornstarch is completely dissolved. Cook on high (600–700 watts) 4–5 minutes, until mixture comes to a boil, stirring twice. Beat egg yolks, stir a little of the pineapple mixture into the egg yolks, mix well, and return to pineapple mixture. Stir in lemon rind, lemon juice, and cream cheese. Continue to cook on high 1 minute. Beat with an electric mixer to blend cream cheese and eggs. Set aside to cool.

When it has cooled, beat egg whites until frothy and gradually add ¼ cup sugar until soft peaks form. Fold into cooled pudding.

Spoon into dessert dishes and refrigerate until ready to serve.

SERVES 4

CREME CARAMEL

This microwave adaptation of a classic French dessert is designed for ovens with low power settings. It is also important to have the proper dish. Since the high temperature needed to caramelize the sugar requires tempered glass, you should use a 1½-quart brioche dish (or other similar fluted dish) made of Pyrex.

> 12 tablespoons sugar, divided
> 2 tablespoons water
> 2 cups milk
> 3 eggs
> 3 egg yolks
> 1 teaspoon vanilla

Combine 6 tablespoons sugar with water in 1½-quart glass brioche dish and blend well. Cook on high (600–700 watts) until mixture just turns brown, about 4 minutes; do not overcook or caramel will be bitter. Remove from microwave and carefully tilt dish to coat bottom and sides evenly.

Pour milk into a 4-cup glass measure and cook on high until scalded, about 3–4 minutes, watching closely so milk does not boil. In 2-quart bowl, whisk together eggs, egg yolks, remaining sugar, and vanilla until well blended. Slowly add hot milk, whisking constantly until thoroughly mixed. Pour into caramelized mixture. Cook on medium (300–350 watts) until custard begins to set, about 17–20 minutes. (Custard is starting to set when it begins to shrink from sides of dish.) Custard will be liquid in center when removed from oven since, like all custards, it will set as it cools. Cool completely.

To serve, run knife along edge of custard before inverting and unmolding on small platter.

SERVES 6–8

Fresh Apples in Custard Sauce
Pears Poached in Red Wine
Caramel Apples
Caramelized Pears
Fresh Fruit Compote
Fluffy Lemon Fruit Dressing
Chocolate-Dipped Fruit
Chocolate Bananas on Sticks
Fruit-Topped Meringue Cups
Chocolate Fondue

4
FRUIT DESSERTS

Something wonderful happens to fruit when it is heated in the microwave. All of the natural flavors are brought out because you need not add any water. It cooks itself until hot and the juices are released, creating a full-bodied sauce.

During the summer, there are so many ways to enjoy variety. Use this method to cook fruit for ice cream sundaes; it is as good as hot fudge.

I like to cook a combination of fruits together. The blending of flavors in the compote is rich and satisfying. If you wish to present a perfectly cooked arrangement, you may wish to cook each fruit separately and then combine them in one bowl.

Many of these recipes can easily become sugar-free without loss of flavor. Simply use your favorite sugar substitute to equal the amount of sugar used in the recipe. Always add it after the cooking process has been completed. (The Fresh Fruit Tart with Orange Glaze and the Lemon Pineapple Cream are also well-suited to sugar substitutions. See index for recipes.)

The easiest way to cook fresh fruit to its maximum flavor is to bring the fruit to the point where the juices are beginning to cover the fruit. Then stir gently with a wooden spoon and set it aside to cool. This takes place at different times for different fruits. A fully ripened peach may cook faster than a firm nectarine or plum. Either way, the results are outstanding, and this is a great way to salvage fresh fruit that has been in the fruit bowl just a bit too long and won't survive another day. Just cook it, add a bit of fruity liquor, and enjoy.

FRESH APPLES IN CUSTARD SAUCE

Apple pie with a slice of cheddar cheese on top inspired this recipe. It is a make-and-serve-now recipe.

> 3 cups sliced (unpeeled) red baking apples
> 1 tablespoon lemon juice
> 2 tablespoons butter
> 1 tablespoon brown sugar
> 1 teaspoon ground cinnamon
> 1½ tablespoons flour

CUSTARD SAUCE

> 2 eggs, beaten
> 1½–2 cups shredded cheddar cheese

For apples: Slice apples, sprinkle with lemon juice, and set aside. In a 1-quart round deep soufflé-type dish, place butter, sugar, and cinnamon. Cook on high (600–700 watts) 1 minute. Stir to blend flavors.

Toss apples in flour and add to melted butter, stirring to coat apples. Cover and cook on high 3 minutes. Stir, cover, and set aside.

For sauce: Whip eggs with wire whisk and blend in cheese. Pour over apples. Cover and cook on medium (300–350 watts) 7 minutes. Serve immediately.

SERVES 4

PEARS POACHED
IN RED WINE

A truly elegant dessert—and just the right touch after a heavy meal. The microwave does this beautifully.

4 firm, ripe pears
3 cups water
3 tablespoons fresh lemon juice
2 cups dry red wine
½ cup sugar
1 cinnamon stick, plus ¼ teaspoon ground cinnamon
Rind of ½ lemon
Mint for garnish (optional)

Peel pears, leaving stems intact. Place in large bowl with water and lemon juice to keep pears from turning dark.

Combine wine, sugar, cinnamon, and lemon rind in a 2-quart round baking dish. Cook on high (600–700 watts) for 5 minutes. Add pears, turning them in the wine to coat completely. Cover with waxed paper and cook on high about 9–10 minutes, until pears are just fork tender. Turn pears once or twice during cooking to keep them nicely colored.

When pears are tender, spoon juices over them while they cool (pears should remain in liquid until ready to serve). Serve at room temperature, or chilled.

Add a piece of mint to the stem before serving.

SERVES 4

CARAMEL APPLES

Much better than store-bought.

1 14-ounce package light caramels
2 tablespoons water
5 wooden sticks
5 medium apples
¾ cup chopped nuts (chopped peanut
    topping in packages is outstanding)
    (optional)

Place unwrapped caramels in a 2-quart glass measure. Add water. Cook on high (600–700 watts) for 3–4 minutes, until softened. Stir until completely melted.

Push a stick into center of each apple. Dip into hot caramel, turning to coat evenly.

If using nut coating, spread nuts on waxed paper and roll apples in mixture. Place apples on buttered waxed paper until cool.

Note: If caramel hardens, you may reheat for 30–45 seconds.

MAKES 5

COLOR PLATES

Plate 1: Almond Layer Cake *(page 29)*
Plate 2: White Chocolate Almond Bark *(page 113)*
        Honeycomb *(page 116)*
        Chocolate-Dipped Fruit *(page 86)*
Plate 3: Kahlua Chocolate Almond Mousse *(page 73)*
Plate 4: Indian Corn *(page 130)*
Plate 5: Perfect Lemon Meringue Pie *(page 52)*
Plate 6: English Trifle *(page 32)*
Plate 7: Fresh Fruit Tart with Orange Glaze *(page 57)*
Plate 8: Chocolate Mousse Layer Cake *(page 20)*

CARAMELIZED PEARS

A caramel glaze to complement a fresh pear. Use firm, ripe pears for good results. Make the glaze first, then poach the pears slightly, add the glaze, and cook until pears are tender.

CARAMEL GLAZE

½ cup dark corn syrup
2 tablespoons brown sugar
1 tablespoon honey
1 tablespoon water
¼ teaspoon maple extract or vanilla

Combine all ingredients in 2-quart glass measure. Cook on high (600–700 watts) 2 minutes, or until syrup comes to a rolling boil. Stir and set aside.

POACHED PEARS

1 cup dry sherry
½ cup water
2 tablespoons lemon juice
4 whole cloves
1 stick cinnamon or ¼ teaspoon ground
    cinnamon
2 firm pears (6–8 ounces each), cut in half

Combine all ingredients except pears in a 2-quart round baking dish. Place pears in baking dish skin side up and cover, cooking for 6–7 minutes on high (600–700 watts). Pears should be firm. Drain liquid from pears and discard. Pour Caramel Glaze over pears. Turn pears skin side down on glaze and cook uncovered for 5 minutes on medium (300–350 watts).

Turn over, cook on high an additional 1–2 minutes. Arrange pears skin side up on serving plate.

Garnish with sprig of mint or chocolate leaf.

SERVES 4

FRESH FRUIT COMPOTE

2 peaches, quartered and pitted
4 apricots, quartered and pitted
4 plums, halved and pitted
10 cherries, halved and pitted
1 small bunch grapes

Combine all ingredients in a 2-quart bowl or cook each fruit separately and then combine in serving bowl. Cook on high (600–700 watts) until juices come to a rolling boil, about 7–9 minutes. Stir gently to coat fruit with the juices. Serve warm or at room temperature. Fruit tastes best at room temperature, not chilled.

VARIATION: ICE CREAM SUNDAE FRUIT TOPPINGS

Have a bowl of fruit on hand and let your guests cook their own toppings!

Cherries, halved and pitted
Peaches, sliced
Plums, sliced
Nectarines, sliced
Apricots, sliced
Apples, cored and sliced or chopped, plus
    a touch of cinnamon

Put fruits in a glass measure bowl of the appropriate size. Cook only until juices come to a rolling boil. Timing will depend on the ripeness and amount of the fruit.

You may cook the fruit right in the serving dish if the dish is microwave-safe, then add a scoop of ice cream.

FLUFFY LEMON
FRUIT DRESSING

This is a fluffy fruit dressing, tangy and different, to serve as a dip with fresh fruits and berries. I discovered it in Marlene Sorosky's Cookery for Entertaining. *She cooked it for 10–15 minutes, but we can do it in the microwave in a fraction of that time.*

This dip may be refrigerated several days. We served it in a bowl in the center of a fresh fruit platter, and it didn't last long.

⅓ cup sugar
1 tablespoon flour
1 teaspoon grated lemon rind
¼ cup lemon juice
1 egg, well beaten
1 cup miniature marshmallows
1 cup dairy sour cream

In a 1-quart glass measure, combine sugar and flour. Stir in lemon rind, lemon juice, and egg, mixing until smooth. Add marshmallows and cook on high (600–700 watts) 2–3½ minutes, until mixture thickens slightly and marshmallows melt. Cool slightly. Stir in sour cream and serve with a variety of fresh fruits and berries.

MAKES 2 CUPS

CHOCOLATE-DIPPED FRUIT

For an attractive presentation, use white and dark chocolate for dipping and use an assortment of fruits and nuts. It is very appealing for parties, gift giving, and small gatherings when you would like to serve something light and different. (See photo.)

Use your imagination in choosing fruits and nuts to dip. In the directions below, we tell you how to handle some of the most popular choices, but feel free to experiment.

> **6 ounces white chocolate or semisweet chocolate bits**
>
> **15–20 large ripe strawberries *or* dried fruit *or* maraschino cherries *or* other jarred fruit *or* whole roasted nuts *or* thin lemon slices**

Place chocolate in a 1-cup glass measure and heat on high (600–700 watts) for 1–2 minutes, just until chocolate turns shiny. Stir until it melts. If not quite melted, place back in microwave for 20–30 seconds.

The following are directions for dipping various fruits and nuts.

Strawberries: Wash and dry the berries, but do not remove their leaves. Prepare them the morning of the day they are to be used or the day before if the berries are quite firm. Line a baking sheet with waxed paper. Hold the strawberry by the leaves and dip it into the melted chocolate (I think they look outstanding dipped only halfway). Place them on the lined baking sheet. Refrigerate until they are firm. To serve, arrange on an attractive serving dish or place each one in its own paper bonbon cup (these can be purchased at party shops).

Dried fruit: Do not wash. Simply dip fruit one at a time in melted chocolate, covering ½ or ¾ of the fruit. Place on lined baking sheet and refrigerate until firm.

Cherries or other fruit in jars: Make certain fruit is completely dry before dipping in chocolate or chocolate will not stick. Dip as for other fruits and refrigerate on lined baking sheet until firm.

Lemon slices: cover thin, halved slices completely in chocolate. Do not refrigerate.

Nuts: Dip as for fruits, covering each nut halfway. Refrigerate on lined baking sheet until firm.

COATS 15-20 STRAWBERRIES, OR OTHER SMALL FRUIT

CHOCOLATE BANANAS ON STICKS

Fun for children's parties or as an afternoon snack.

5 large firm bananas, peeled and cut in half crosswise

10 wooden skewers

1 6-ounce package semisweet chocolate chips

If bananas are small, just cut a small piece off one end. Insert a stick into center of the cut end of banana.

Place chocolate in 4-cup glass measure. Melt on high (600–700 watts) for 1½–2 minutes, just until chocolate becomes shiny (it will not melt until stirred).

Stir and pour small amounts of chocolate over bananas, coating all sides well. Place on baking sheet and keep in freezer until ready to serve.

MAKES 10

FRUIT-TOPPED MERINGUE CUPS

One of the first uniquely microwave fun things we learned was soft meringue. I don't know about you, but it never fails to disappoint me when I order a beautiful dessert, displayed on a dessert cart, with baked meringue holding a filling of some type.

If you are willing to adopt the microwave mentality of enjoying the pure white, luscious, soft texture without a preconceived notion of how it must look, you will find that this type of recipe will become a family favorite.

> ½ cup egg whites
> ¼ teaspoon cream of tartar
> ⅓ cup sugar
> ½ teaspoon vanilla
> ⅛ teaspoon ground ginger
> Whipped cream
> Fresh fruit (an assortment of strawberries, blueberries, sliced peaches, apricots, and kiwifruit)
> 6 sprigs mint for garnish

With an electric mixer, in a medium-sized bowl, beat egg whites and cream of tartar until soft peaks form. While beating, slowly add sugar until stiff, but not dry. Beat in vanilla and ginger.

Spoon meringue onto sheet of waxed paper in six equal swirls, arranged in a circle. Using back of a spoon, indent center of each to make a cup. Cook on high (600–700 watts) for 3–5 minutes, just until firm but still moist. Allow to cool before filling with a spoonful of whipped cream, fresh fruit, and a dollop of whipped cream on top. Garnish with a fresh sprig of mint.

For an attractive presentation, place a doily on a dessert plate, place meringue shell on top, then fill with filling. Place a Cracked Gingersnap (see index) on each dessert plate.

SERVES 6

CHOCOLATE FONDUE

A fun way to serve fresh fruit. Each person selects a chunk of fruit and, using a fondue fork, regular fork, or long wooden skewer, dips it into the warm chocolate. You could also serve pastry chunks or an assortment of both fruit and pastry.

1 12-ounce package semisweet chocolate
  bits
3 ounces baking chocolate
½ cup heavy cream
2 tablespoons Kahlua (optional)

Place all ingredients in an attractive bowl suitable for serving. Heat on high (600–700 watts) for 2–2½ minutes, until chocolate appears shiny. Stir until smooth. Serve immediately. If reheating is necessary, use medium (300–350 watts).

You can also melt the mixture in the microwave and transfer it to a fondue pot.

SERVES 4–6

Light Citrus Dessert
Lemon Ice Cream
Banana Sherbet
Apple Sherbet
Orange Sherbet
Avocado-Lime Sherbet
Fresh Cantaloupe Sherbet

5
SHERBETS

Sherbets and ices, once served at royal dinners to cleanse the palate between courses, are now commonly served as desserts. An ice is simply frozen fruit juice, sugar, and water. A sherbet differs from an ice in that it has added milk or egg whites. Ice cream, on the other hand, is frozen cream, sugar, and flavoring. All are whipped during the freezing process to keep them light. The best results are produced when the fruit is frozen and whipped several times before serving.

In finer restaurants, sherbet is always rewhipped to lighten the texture by incorporating air. This can be done at home with a food processor, blender, or mixer. If you are serving it immediately after making it, this may not be necessary. However, sherbets and ices made at home do not contain the emulsifiers or stabilizers that commercial products do, so they will crystallize after several days. You can eliminate the crystals by partially thawing the sherbets or ices and rewhipping as you serve or several hours before serving.

Fresh sherbets are quite simple to make. The difference between an outstanding and an ordinary taste, aside from the ingredients, is the texture. No matter how good the recipe, it will not fill your mouth with pleasure unless you take the time to fluff it again in a food processor, mixer, or blender. This removes the icicles that form and gives it the creamy, soft texture. To make this easy to accomplish, freeze it in a mixing bowl. If you have a hand mixer, you can rewhip it right in the bowl when it becomes crystallized.

If you plan to store the product in your freezer, you can use metal ice cube trays with the dividers removed, metal bowls, or shallow cake pans. When it hardens around the edges but is still soft in the middle (after approximately two hours), it is ready to be rewhipped. Or it can be left frozen until ready to serve, then whipped and spooned into serving dishes. When storing sherbets in the freezer, use airtight covered containers. One hour before serving, remove from freezer and place in refrigerator for optimum flavor and texture.

Although there are formulas for preparing sherbets and ices, I have followed the trend to cut down the sugar. The amount of sugar and liquid can vary with each recipe. Freezing diminishes the intensity of sweeteners, so you may wish to experiment to determine the amount of sweetness that appeals to you.

Excellent flavors are developed when using a syrup, which is first cooked to dissolve the sugar, then cooled before combining it with other ingredients. Syrups can be made ahead of time in your microwave in a 4-cup glass measure, then stored in your refrigerator indefinitely. As a general rule, the syrup should be made with equal portions of water and sugar. Use ⅔ cup water and ⅔ cup sugar for 1 cup syrup.

The basic sherbet calls for about 1 cup syrup for 3 cups of fruit. There may be exceptions to this with some fruits.

Liqueurs may be used to make a dessert sherbet, such as raspberry liqueur with frozen or fresh raspberries. Liquid should be reduced accordingly.

Egg whites, whipping cream, or yogurt can also be added to the sherbet for texture. Whatever ingredients you choose, make sure they are chilled before mixing and freezing.

LIGHT CITRUS DESSERT

Unflavored gelatin can contribute to lower calories, while still giving us that creamy texture that satisfies those cravings for a rich dessert. This recipe was developed by Sunkist during the 1984 Olympics in Los Angeles, and each serving contains only 167 calories. All I did was change the cooking procedure to suit the microwave.

> 2 tablespoons (2 envelopes) unflavored
>   gelatin
> 1¾ cups water, divided
> ¾ cup sugar, divided
> Grated rind of 1 lemon
> ½ cup fresh lemon juice
> 2 egg whites

Soften gelatin in ¼ cup water. In a 4-cup glass measure, combine ½ cup sugar and remaining 1½ cups water. Cook on high (600–700 watts) for 4–5 minutes (it should remain at a boil for 2 minutes). Stir in gelatin mixture until it dissolves. Add lemon rind and juice. Pour into shallow 8″ pan. Freeze just until slushy (about 1½ hours), stirring occasionally. Beat egg whites until foamy. Gradually add remaining ¼ cup sugar, beating until soft peaks form. Fold beaten egg whites into lemon mixture. Return to freezer; stir occasionally. Freeze until firm (about 4 hours).

MAKES SEVEN ½-CUP SERVINGS

LEMON ICE CREAM

This recipe is rich and creamy, with the natural flavor provided by fresh lemons, and is for those who own an ice cream maker. An alternative would be to use fresh oranges or grapefruit.

> **1 cup whipping cream**
> **1 cup milk**
> **1 cup sugar**
> **Juice and grated rind of 2 lemons**
> **Oranges and lemons for serving**
> **Sprigs of fresh mint for garnish**

In a 2-quart glass measure, place cream, milk, and sugar. Heat on high (600–700 watts) for 5–7 minutes, stirring twice, until sugar is dissolved and mixture is hot. Set aside to cool.

Add lemon juice and lemon rind. Pour mixture into freezer can and freeze by following instructions that come with your ice cream maker.

To serve, hollow out a large lemon or orange. Place lemon ice cream inside and add a sprig of fresh mint.

Note: Orange, lemon, and grapefruit shells can be accumulated by storing the shells in your freezer each time you use the fruit for other recipes.

MAKES 1 QUART

BANANA SHERBET

> **⅔ cup sugar**
> **⅔ cup water**
> **2 large firm, ripe bananas, sliced**
> **1 cup fresh orange juice**
> **1 tablespoon fresh lemon juice**
> **Raspberry Sauce (see index)**

Combine sugar and water in 2-cup glass measure. Cook on high (600–700 watts) 3–4 minutes, until sugar is dissolved. Stir, allow to cool, then cover and chill.

Place bananas on a shallow tray. Place in freezer until partially frozen. Place in blender and puree. Add cooled syrup and juices and blend until combined. Place in freezer, covered, until ready to serve. Rewhip and spoon into hollowed-out orange halves. Serve with Raspberry Sauce.

MAKES ABOUT 4 CUPS

AVOCADO-LIME SHERBET

Hollowed-out lime halves, garnished with mint, are the perfect "dishes" for serving this sherbet.

⅔ **cup sugar**
⅔ **cup water**
2 large ripe avocados, peeled
¼ **cup fresh lime juice**
1 drop hot pepper sauce
Pinch salt

Combine sugar and water in 2-cup glass measure. Cook on high (600–700 watts) for 3–4 minutes, until sugar dissolves. Stir and allow to cool. Cover and chill.

Cut avocado into pieces. Place in blender with remaining ingredients and blend well. Place in a metal bowl and chill in freezer until partially frozen.

Combine chilled syrup with chilled avocado puree in blender. Process until smooth. Freeze in shallow containers. When ready to serve, remove from freezer, allow to soften slightly, and rewhip before spooning into lime halves or serving dishes.

MAKES ABOUT 3 CUPS

APPLE SHERBET

1 cup apple juice
½ cup sugar
4 apples, peeled, cored, and cut into small
   pieces
¼ cup lemon juice
2 tablespoons applejack (optional)
Pinch ground nutmeg
Pinch ground cinnamon

Place apple juice and sugar in a 2-quart bowl. Cook on high (600–700 watts) until sugar dissolves, about 4–5 minutes. Stir. Add apples and lemon juice and cook, covered, on high until apples are soft, about 3–5 minutes. Stir and allow to cool. Stir in applejack and spices. Place bowl in freezer. When ready to serve, remove amount needed and whip in blender just before placing in serving dishes. (This may be done about an hour ahead of time by placing the serving dishes in the freezer.)

MAKES ABOUT 3 CUPS

ORANGE SHERBET

No cooking for this one, but I wanted to share it with you.

2 large oranges
½ cup frozen orange juice concentrate
2 tablespoons cream or milk

With a potato peeler (or a zester, if you own one), remove orange rind (outer colored portion without the white part). If using the peeler, mince the rind. Remove white section from oranges and cut oranges into chunks. (Do this on a flat plate so that you can save any juices that are released when cutting.)

Place orange pieces and any juices in blender with the frozen orange juice concentrate, milk, and minced rind. Mix well. Place in freezer until partially frozen. Whip it well and return to freezer, covered, until ready to serve. Whip again just before serving.

For an attractive presentation, spoon sherbet into orange halves with pulp scooped out.

MAKES ABOUT 4 CUPS

FRESH CANTALOUPE SHERBET

⅔ cup sugar
⅔ cup water
4 cups peeled and chopped very ripe
    cantaloupe
2 tablespoons fresh lemon juice
Rind of lemon, minced
Pinch ground cinnamon
2 tablespoons cream
Cantaloupe wedges for serving

Combine sugar and water in 2-cup glass measure. Cook on high (600–700 watts) 3–4 minutes, until sugar is dissolved. Stir, allow to cool, then cover and chill in freezer.

Place chopped cantaloupe, lemon juice, lemon rind, and cinnamon in blender. Puree mixture and add cooled syrup and cream. Blend again.

Freeze in shallow container until ready to serve. Remove from freezer, allow to soften slightly, and rewhip before spooning into cantaloupe wedges to serve. (You may do this an hour before serving and place wedges in freezer.)

MAKES ABOUT 4 CUPS

Cracked Gingersnaps
Cocoa Cookies
Fortune Cookies
Chocolate Mousse Brownies
Lemon Bars

6
COOKIES AND BROWNIES

Most microwave cooks would agree that the preparation of cookies is best left to conventional ovens because you can bake two cookie trays at once. However, there are some cookies that are especially well-suited to the microwave. Delicious and a delight to make, these recipes are guaranteed to bring out the kid in everybody.

CRACKED GINGERSNAPS

A number of years ago, a beautiful book was developed by five Hartford, Connecticut, arts organizations. They invited me to review the manuscript and adapt those recipes to the microwave that were suitable. Naturally, I was flattered to be chosen and excited about many of the fine contributions made by these talented women, who obviously loved food as well as the arts. Each of them donated treasured recipes and gave away culinary secrets.

Although cookies are not usually successful in the microwave, and it doesn't make sense to make a few at a time when you can place a full tray in a regular oven, I was tempted to test the Cracked Gingersnaps. I love the odor of ginger in my kitchen. It reminds me of when my sister and I were growing up and my mother made a special ginger treat for us at certain holidays.

Lo and behold, the cookies were an immediate success, and I make them often—especially in the summer, when the last thing in the world I would do is turn on my oven. In the San Fernando Valley, our air conditioning is good only up to a point!

¾ cup shortening
1 cup brown sugar
4 tablespoons molasses
1 egg
2 cups flour
2 teaspoons baking soda
1 teaspoon ground cinnamon
1 teaspoon ground cloves
1 teaspoon ground ginger
½ teaspoon salt
Extra granulated sugar for coating

Cream shortening and sugar in mixing bowl. Add molasses and egg, beating well. Blend dry ingredients together (except extra sugar), add to batter, and mix by hand until smooth. The batter will be stiff. Refrigerate batter at least 2 hours.

To bake, form chilled batter into 1-inch balls. Roll in granulated sugar and place 12 balls 3 inches apart in a circle on a sheet of parchment paper placed on the bottom of your microwave. Do not press the cookie dough; just leave it in the shape of a ball, and it will spread out as it cooks.

Cook on medium (300–350 watts) for 5 minutes. The cookies will be slightly soft but will become quite firm as they cool. Repeat with remaining batter.

If you wish, you may keep the dough covered in the refrigerator for a few days and bake them fresh each day. What a treat for children arriving home from school to share some freshly baked cookies from their very own mix from the refrigerator!

MAKES 50-60 COOKIES

COCOA COOKIES

You may make the dough ahead of time and refrigerate—then microwave these delectable treats only as you need them. The dough can be wrapped tightly in plastic wrap and refrigerated for up to 3 days.

¾ cup (1½ sticks) butter or margarine at
    room temperature
¾ cup sugar
1 egg
1¾ cups flour
¼ cup unsweetened cocoa powder
1 teaspoon baking powder
½ teaspoon salt
1 teaspoon vanilla
½ cup chopped walnuts
Sugar for coating

Combine butter, sugar, and egg in an electric mixer and blend until the mixture is light and fluffy. In a bowl, mix together flour, cocoa, baking powder, and salt; mix until everything is blended. Put the dry mixture into the butter mixture and beat together, just until it is mixed. Do not overbeat. Stir in vanilla and nuts.

Divide dough and roll into 1-inch balls. Put a little sugar into a plate. Roll the balls in the sugar. Place in a dish and cover. Leave in the refrigerator until ready to bake.

To bake, place balls of dough 1½ inches apart on a paper plate. Flatten tops slightly with a spoon. Cook on high (600–700 watts) until cookies are puffed: about 1 minute for 2 cookies; 1¼ minutes for 4 cookies; 2 minutes for 8 cookies; and 3 minutes for 12 cookies. For crisper cookies, let cook an additional few seconds. Let cool slightly before removing from plate (they will get firm as they stand). Transfer to rack and cool completely.

MAKES ABOUT 30 COOKIES

FORTUNE COOKIES

Have fun at a party by having personalized fortunes for the guests and the occasion. Write fortunes on thin paper strips, 3" × ¾".

Gather some helpers, since you must work quickly when cookies are removed from the microwave—they cool and harden rapidly.

> 1 extra-large egg white
> ¼ cup sugar
> ¼ cup flour
> 1 teaspoon very finely chopped blanched almonds
> ½ teaspoon vanilla
> ⅛ teaspoon salt
> 2 tablespoons melted butter

Combine egg white and sugar in small bowl and mix until sugar is dissolved. Stir in each of the remaining ingredients separately and beat until well blended.

Drop dough by level teaspoonfuls far apart onto a shallow baking dish. Bake 9 cookies on high (600–700 watts) for about 3–3½ minutes. Repeat with remaining batter.

One at a time, remove cookies from baking sheet. Place a fortune in center of each, fold over in half, and pinch sides together. They should resemble nurses' caps. Work very quickly since cookies cool and harden rapidly. (If cookies harden before filling, reheat in microwave for 10–15 seconds.)

MAKES 12-16 COOKIES

CHOCOLATE MOUSSE BROWNIES

When you have a good brownie recipe and an absolutely fail-safe chocolate mousse done in the microwave, what better way to enjoy it than to double your pleasure?

BROWNIE

2 ounces unsweetened baking chocolate
½ cup (1 stick) butter or margarine
2 eggs
¾ cup sugar
½ cup flour
1 teaspoon baking powder
¼ teaspoon salt
1 teaspoon vanilla
1 cup coarsely chopped walnuts
1 cup chocolate chips

MOUSSE

4 ounces semisweet chocolate
1 ounce baking chocolate
15 large marshmallows
½ cup milk
1 tablespoon unsweetened cocoa powder
1 teaspoon vanilla

For brownies: Combine baking chocolate and butter in a 2-cup glass measure. Cook on high (600–700 watts) until butter is melted, about 1½ minutes. Stir to blend butter and chocolate (chocolate will not appear melted until you stir). Set chocolate mixture aside.

Beat eggs in large bowl until well mixed. Add remaining brownie ingredients and stir until well blended. Add chocolate mixture. Blend well.

Turn into a 9″ pie plate or quiche dish. Cook on high 6 minutes. Mixture will still be moist but will firm as it cools. Set aside and make mousse.

For mousse: Combine all ingredients except vanilla in a 1-quart glass measure. Cook on high for about 2–2½ minutes, stirring once, just until marshmallows are melted. Stir in vanilla.

Set aside to cool slightly. It will thicken as it cools. When it has cooled down and is beginning to thicken, spoon it on the brownie. Cut into 16 pieces. If not served, cover and refrigerate. May be frozen. (Place in freezer without wrapping. When it has completely frozen, wrap for freezer. This will keep the mousse from sticking to the freezer paper.)

MAKES 16 BROWNIES

LEMON BARS

This is my son Paul's recipe. When there is nothing "good" to eat in the cookie jar, he can prepare these fast. They have a nice lemon flavor and are delicious to share with friends with a glass of milk.

CRUST

½ cup (1 stick) butter or margarine, softened
1 cup flour
⅓ cup confectioners' (powdered) sugar

FILLING

2 eggs
1 cup sugar
1½ teaspoons cornstarch
½ teaspoon baking powder
1 tablespoon lemon rind, grated
3½ tablespoons lemon juice
Confectioners' (powdered) sugar to sprinkle on top

For crust: Place butter or margarine in a 9″ round microwave baking dish. Place in the microwave on high (600–700 watts) for 45 seconds to soften. Combine flour and sugar and add to butter; stir all ingredients together until mixture is crumbly. Press the mixture into the bottom of the dish. Cook on high 4 minutes. Set crust aside while you prepare the filling.

For filling: In a 1-quart glass measure, combine the eggs and sugar; beat until mixture is fluffy. Add all the rest of the ingredients and stir well until the cornstarch is completely dissolved.

Pour this mixture over the baked crust. Cook on high for 3½–4½ minutes, just until the center begins to look set. Remove from microwave and let stand at least 10 minutes before cutting so that the custard can set completely.

Sprinkle powdered sugar over the top and cut into 12-16 bars.

MAKES 12-16 BARS

White Almond Bark with White Raisins
Chocolate Almond Bark
Penuche
Peppermint Divinity
Honeycomb
Kahlua Cream Truffles
Fantasy Fudge
Kahlua Fudge
Crispy Caramel Marshmallows
Chocolate-Covered Marshmallows
Almond Cream Candy
Cinnamon/Spice Nuts
Peanut Brittle
Turkish Delight
Perfectly Nutty Chocolate Bar
Lollipops
Rocky Road
Chocolate Cups
Chocolate Bonbon Cups
Indian Corn

7
CANDIES AND NUTS

Candy Made Easy

Microwave cooking has taken the mystery out of candy-making, and budding chocolatiers no longer have to spend hours slaving over a hot stove to produce tasty results that are better than store-bought.

Perhaps the greatest advantage of the microwave for candy-making is the absence of direct heat. There is less chance of overcooking or scorching, the most frequent pitfalls of the novice. Microwave heat is more uniform (around top, bottom, and sides of bowl), and since microwave energy keeps the mixture constantly in motion, there is no need to stir continually as required for many conventional candy recipes (usually over a double boiler).

Temperature and the ratio of ingredients are important factors in both conventional and microwave candy-making. The temperature of the basic syrup controls the moisture content of the finished candy, which in turn determines its characteristics, such as the difference between taffy and peanut brittle. Microwave cooking does not reduce moisture as quickly as conventional cooking, and since reducing moisture is the key to success, it is sometimes a good idea to cut back a bit on the amount of water specified when adapting your favorite recipes to microwave.

You will also find that most of my microwave recipes use sugar and corn syrup in combination. Corn syrup controls crystalization and gives more flexibility in timing when a thermometer is not available. It contains sugar in the form of dextrose and maltose, which do not crystalize readily yet do interfere with the crystalization of other sugars.

Candy-Making Tips

- Use the 2-quart heat-proof measuring cup for preparing candy. The handle stays cool even though the sugar mixture is very hot, so you can remove it from the microwave at just the right moment.
- Simple cleanup: If the syrup remaining in the measuring cup hardens before washing, add some water to it and bring to a boil in microwave on high (600–700 watts). Any sticky nonmetal utensils can be added to the cup and cleaned at the same time.

Testing the Temperature

New candy thermometers designed for microwave use take the guesswork out of preparation. But if you don't want to invest in one, here is a standard test to determine the approximate temperature and firmness of candy mixtures:

Drop a small amount of the boiling syrup into a cup of very cold water (without ice), being sure to take the remaining candy mixture out of the microwave during testing to prevent overcooking. Shape syrup gently with fingertips, then remove from water.

Soft Ball (234-240°F)

Shapes into soft ball that flattens when removed from water.

Firm Ball (244-248°F)

Shapes into firm ball that does not flatten when removed from water.

Hard Ball (250-255°F)

Forms ball that is hard enough to hold its shape but is still pliable.

Soft Crack (270-290°F)

Syrup separates into threads that are hard but not brittle.

Hard Crack (300-310°F)

Syrup separates into hard and brittle threads.

WHITE ALMOND BARK WITH WHITE RAISINS

The store-bought version of this confection costs about $25 a pound. I can never allow myself to buy enough to be satisfied, so I make it myself.

An outstanding Swiss confectionery bar of white chocolate is made by Chocolate Tobler of Switzerland. I have found it across the country. It is a long, narrow bar, in a triangle-shaped white box with red letters. It is made with almond and honey nougat and is a taste experience you won't soon forget. It makes the best bark in the world. If you cannot locate it, substitute a good-quality white chocolate.

> 4 3.52-ounce bars Swiss Toblerone
> (white chocolate with almond and
> honey nougat)
> 1 cup blanched whole almonds
> 1 teaspoon butter
> 1 cup white raisins

Break chocolate into pieces and place in a 2-quart bowl. Set aside. Combine almonds and butter in a 9″ pie plate and cook on high (600–700 watts), stirring once or twice, until almonds are toasted, about 4–5 minutes. Set aside.

Line baking sheet with waxed paper and set aside. Melt chocolate on high 1½–2 minutes, just until it appears shiny. Remember, it will not change shape and melt until you stir. Do not overcook or chocolate will become grainy. If not quite melted, cook 30 seconds more. Stir in almonds and raisins and blend well. Immediately spread mixture on waxed paper to the desired thickness. Allow to set. Break into pieces to serve. May be refrigerated.

MAKES ABOUT 1½ POUNDS

CHOCOLATE ALMOND BARK

Some people think this is the ultimate, pure way to enjoy chocolate. If you break it into large pieces, it will have more impact; everyone will take seconds anyway.

For white chocolate bark, simply use a white chocolate base.

> 1 cup blanched whole almonds
> 1 tablespoon butter
> 1 pound good-quality chocolate,
>   broken into pieces

Combine the almonds and butter in an 8″ pie plate. Cook on high (600–700 watts), stirring several times, until the almonds are toasted, about 4–5 minutes. Stir again and leave in plate to cool.

Line a baking sheet with waxed paper and set aside. Melt the chocolate pieces in a 2-quart bowl on high just until chocolate turns shiny (it will not melt until stirred), about 1½–2½ minutes. Do not overcook, or the chocolate will become grainy.

Stir in the almonds and blend well. Immediately spread the mixture onto the baking sheet. Refrigerate until set. Break into pieces to serve.

For gift giving, it is most impressive to leave bark whole.

MAKES ABOUT 1 POUND

PENUCHE

1 pound light brown sugar
1 tablespoon light corn syrup
1 tablespoon butter
¾ cup evaporated milk
1 teaspoon vanilla
⅔ cup chopped pecans or walnuts

In a 2-quart glass measure, combine sugar, corn syrup, butter, and evaporated milk. Stir until well mixed. Cook on high (600–700 watts) until mixture reaches the soft ball stage (234–240°F on a candy thermometer), about 7 minutes. Allow to cool to about 120°F. Stir in vanilla and nuts. Beat until mixture thickens and begins to lose its gloss. Turn into greased 8″ × 8″ pan. Mark into squares and cut when cold. Pieces may be wrapped in waxed paper, foil, or cellophane.

MAKES ABOUT 1¼ POUNDS

PEPPERMINT DIVINITY

A refreshing, light candy that is great for holiday giving. This may be made ahead of time, refrigerated, and served to guests, or pieces may be wrapped individually in cellophane and placed in a festive box as a gift to someone who appreciates quality candy.

It is important to have an electric mixer to complete the candy, since the light texture achieved with egg whites needs time to develop. Without an electric mixer, you'll need more time and a srong arm.

2⅔ cups sugar
⅔ cup light corn syrup
½ cup water
3 egg whites
¼ teaspoon peppermint flavoring
1 cup chopped or slivered almonds
1 cup crushed peppermint candy
3-4 drops red food coloring

Combine sugar, corn syrup, and water in 2-quart bowl. Cook on high (600–700 watts) until candy thermometer registers 260°F (or until a small amount of mixture forms ball hard enough to hold its shape, but still pliable, when dropped into bowl of very cold water), about 12–15 minutes.

Beat egg whites until stiff. Gradually pour hot syrup into egg whites, beating constantly. Add peppermint flavoring and chopped or slivered almonds and continue beating until candy is stiff and loses its gloss. Mix in crushed candy and food coloring. Drop by teaspoonfuls onto waxed paper. Cool completely before storing in airtight container in cool place.

MAKES ABOUT 3 DOZEN PIECES

HONEYCOMB

1 cup sugar
1 cup dark corn syrup
1 tablespoon white vinegar
1 tablespoon baking soda

CHOCOLATE COATING

1 12-ounce package semisweet real
  chocolate chips
3 tablespoons solid vegetable shortening
1 ounce (1 square) unsweetened baking
  chocolate, broken into small pieces

Line 8″ × 8″ baking dish with foil; grease generously and
set aside. Combine sugar, corn syrup, and vinegar in 2-quart
bowl and cook on high (600–700 watts) 3 minutes. Stir through
several times. Continue cooking on high until mixture has
thickened and candy thermometer registers 300°F (or until
small amount of mixture separates into hard and brittle threads
when dropped into very cold water), about 7–10 minutes.
Quickly stir in baking soda (mixture will foam), blending
completely. Pour into baking dish, tilting to cover bottom
evenly. Let cool at room temperature until firm, about 1 hour
(do not refrigerate). Break honeycomb into pieces and set aside.

Combine chocolate chips, shortening, and baking chocolate in a 2-quart bowl; cook on high 2 minutes. Using wooden
spoon, stir through to melt thoroughly. (Chocolate will not
appear melted until stirred; do not cook chocolate, just heat
long enough to soften.) Dip honeycomb pieces into chocolate,
covering completely. Place on waxed paper. Let cool at room
temperature.

MAKES ABOUT 1 POUND

KAHLUA CREAM
TRUFFLES

Chocolate cases or cups are fun to prepare and easier to make than you think. They will impress your guests when you fill them with these truffles.

> **8 ounces white chocolate**
> **¼ cup Kahlua**
> **¼ cup butter**
> **Chocolate Bonbon Cups (see index)**

Break chocolate into pieces and place in a 2-quart glass measure. Add Kahlua and butter. Melt on high (600–700 watts) for 1½–2½ minutes, just until chocolate turns shiny. Stir until completely melted and smooth. It will thicken as it cools. If you have a pastry tube, press mixture through large rosette tube into the prepared Chocolate Bonbon Cups and chill until set. If you do not have a pastry tube, a small spoon or knife can be used to fill the centers. Place filled cups in freezer until set.

MAKES ABOUT 30

FANTASY FUDGE

When a student asked me to adapt for the microwave a famous candy store's fudge recipe, that her mother had in her files, I was delighted. After bringing the ingredients home from the market, I discovered the recipe she had given me was on the label of the Kraft Marshmallow Creme jar.

The advantage of cooking it in your microwave? The original version requires constant stirring, until a candy thermometer reaches 234°F, to prevent scorching. No problem for the microwave: no stirring and no scorching! Rich and creamy—great for holiday giving.

> 3 cups sugar
> ¾ cup butter or margarine
> 1 5⅓-ounce can evaporated milk
> 1 12-ounce package semisweet chocolate
>   chips
> 1 7-ounce jar marshmallow cream
> 1 cup chopped nuts
> 1 teaspoon vanilla

Combine sugar, butter, and milk in 2-quart glass measure or bowl that can tolerate high heat. Cook on high (600–700 watts) 7–10 minutes or until a microwave candy thermometer reaches 234°F. If you do not have a microwave candy thermometer, remove bowl from microwave and test with regular candy thermometer.

Stir in chocolate until melted. Add marshmallow cream, nuts, and vanilla; beat until well blended. Pour into a greased 13″ × 9″ pan. Cool at room temperature. Cut into squares.

MAKES 3 POUNDS

KHALUA FUDGE

The easiest fudge recipe I have used, this one is similar to a rocky road. When invited for dinner, prepare it as a gift for the host. Instead of pouring into a utility dish, use an attractive 8" or 9" serving dish that will double as a house gift for your host. Let the fudge cool on the dish and wrap it with cellophane from underneath the dish. Pull the cellophane ends up over the dish and tie with a bow.

> 1 pound confectioners' (powdered) sugar
> 1 cup unsweetened cocoa powder
> ¼ cup milk
> ¼ cup Kahlua
> ¼ pound (1 stick) butter or margarine
> 1 cup walnuts
> 2 cups miniature marshmallows
> 2 teaspoons vanilla

Place sugar, cocoa, milk, Kahlua, and butter in a 2-quart bowl. Cook on high (600–700 watts) for 2–2½ minutes. Stir well to blend ingredients completely. Stir in walnuts, marshmallows, and vanilla. Immediately pour into a lightly greased 8" dish and allow to cool completely in refrigerator before cutting into squares.

MAKES ABOUT 1½ POUNDS

Covered Marshmallow Candy

For some of us, there is something special about biting through chocolate or caramel coatings and discovering a soft marshmallow inside. Here are some suggestions; I am certain you will come up with many more on your own.

CRISPY CARAMEL MARSHMALLOWS

½ cup sweetened condensed milk
½ cup butter
27 caramels
1 10-ounce package large marshmallows
2 cups (approximately) crisp rice cereal

In a 2-quart glass measure, combine milk and butter. Cook on high (600–700 watts) for 1½–2 minutes, stirring once, just long enough to melt the butter.

Stir in caramels and continue to cook on high 1½–2 minutes, stirring frequently to keep sauce smooth.

Using a fork to pierce marshmallows, dip into caramel sauce, then roll in rice cereal to coat outside.

Place on waxed paper and allow to cool completely. Keep covered and refrigerated until ready to use.

MAKES 40 TREATS

CHOCOLATE-COVERED MARSHMALLOWS

1 12-ounce package semisweet chocolate morsels
1 10-ounce package large marshmallows
Walnut halves for garnish (optional)

Place sheet of waxed paper on baking sheet to cool marshmallows after coating. In a 1-quart glass measure, place chocolate pieces. Melt on high (600–700 watts) 1–1½ minutes, just until chocolate turns shiny (it will not melt until you stir). Stir until melted. If not completely melted, place back in microwave for 30 seconds.

With a fork to hold the marshmallow, coat each one with a thick or thin coating, depending on your taste. Place on waxed paper and place a walnut half in center of the marshmallow. Allow to cool.

MAKES 40 TREATS

ALMOND CREAM CANDY

1½ cups sugar
½ cup sour cream
2 cups whole natural almonds
1 tablespoon vanilla

Place a large sheet of foil on a flat tray or cookie sheet.

Combine sugar and sour cream in a 2-quart glass measure. Cook on high (600–700 watts) for 6–7 minutes, stirring every 3 minutes.

Stir in nuts and vanilla and, working quickly, stir to coat almonds and immediately pour onto foil. Allow to cool, then break into pieces. Candy will become crisp. Store in tightly closed container.

MAKES ABOUT 1¼ POUNDS

CINNAMON/SPICE NUTS

2 cups (8 ounces) pecan or walnut halves
1 large egg white (about 2 tablespoons)
¼ cup firmly packed brown sugar
½ teaspoon ground cinnamon
½ teaspoon ground nutmeg

Place nuts and egg white in small bowl. Stir until nuts are well moistened. In a separate bowl, combine remaining ingredients. Mix well, add to nut halves, and stir until well coated.

Spoon into lightly greased 9″ pie plate. Cook on high (600–700 watts) 6–9 minutes or until coating is no longer glossy, stirring once or twice during cooking. Allow to cool before storing in airtight container.

MAKES ABOUT 1 POUND

PEANUT BRITTLE

1 cup sugar
½ cup light corn syrup
¼ cup water
2 cups dry-roasted unsalted peanuts
1 tablespoon butter
1 teaspoon vanilla
1 teaspooon baking soda

Grease large baking sheet. Combine sugar, corn syrup, and water in 2-quart glass measure. Cook on high (600–700 watts) 5 minutes.

Stir in peanuts, using wooden spoon. Continue cooking 5–7 minutes, until temperature reaches 300°F on a candy thermometer or small amount of mixture dropped into very cold water separates into hard and brittle threads.

Stir in butter and vanilla. Stir well, then stir in baking soda. Mixture will become light and foamy. Quickly pour onto prepared sheet, quickly spreading to edges of sheet with back of wooden spoon. As candy cools, stretch into thin sheet using buttered palms of hands.

Let cool completely. Break into pieces and store in cool place.

MAKES ABOUT 1 POUND

TURKISH DELIGHT

The gelatin candies that come from the Middle East, dusted with powdered sugar, are quite easy to duplicate. Using the 2-quart glass measure works well, and the mixture will not boil over because you use a simmer setting.

Some ideas for flavors and fillings: chopped nuts (¼ cup), other citrus juices and rind, any food coloring. Pineapple is not recommended.

> **1 cup water, divided**
> **3 tablespoons (3 envelopes) unflavored gelatin**
> **2 cups sugar**
> **Juice of 1 orange (about ⅓ cup)**
> **Grated rind of 1 orange**
> **Confectioners' (powdered) sugar**

Put ½ cup water into a 1-cup glass measure. Add gelatin, stir to dissolve, and set aside.

Put ½ cup water into a 2-quart glass measure. Stir in sugar. Cook on high (600–700 watts) 5 minutes. Stir in the gelatin mixture and stir well. Cook on high 3 minutes to bring it to a boil. Reduce microwave power to medium (300–350 watts) and simmer for 20 minutes. Strain orange juice into bowl and add the rind.

Pour into a shallow pan large enough for the mixture to be 1 inch deep. Stir in chopped nuts or any other addition desired. Allow to cool slightly before placing it in the refrigerator to cool. When firm, turn it out onto a board that has been dusted with confectioners' sugar. Roll each piece in confectioners' sugar.

MAKES 40–60 PIECES

PERFECTLY NUTTY CHOCOLATE BAR

We experimented—willingly—with many different combinations to come up with the perfect candy bar. We think we've found it in this incredible creation.

> **1 pound semisweet, good-quality chocolate, divided**
> **1 cup salted peanuts**
> **1 cup miniature marshmallows**
> **8 ounces caramels (about 24)**
> **2 tablespoons water**

In a 1-quart glass measure, melt ½ pound chocolate for 2–2½ minutes on high (600–700 watts), or until the chocolate turns shiny. Stir until smooth. Mix in nuts and marshmallows. Turn onto waxed paper. With back of wooden spoon, shape into 4 loglike bars.

In a 2-cup glass measure, combine unwrapped caramels and 2 tablespoons water. Melt for 2 minutes on high. Stir until smooth. Pour equal amounts over the top of each bar.

Melt remaining ½ pound chocolate for 2–2½ minutes on high, stirring until smooth. Pour over each bar, covering completely. Let stand at room temperature for at least 1 hour. Refrigerate until firm before cutting.

MAKES 4 LARGE BARS OR 8 SMALL BARS

LOLLIPOPS

Did you know that the lollipop was introduced in New Haven, Connecticut, in 1908 and was named for a popular racehorse of the day?

½ cup water
1 cup sugar
⅓ cup plus 1 tablespoon light corn syrup
2 teaspoons butter
3 teaspoons flavoring, such as butterscotch, root beer, etc.
Food coloring (optional)
Lollipop sticks or popsicle sticks

Prepare baking sheet, parchment paper, or lollipop molds by brushing with butter. Arrange lollipop sticks on surface, leaving enough space between sticks so that when lollipops are poured they will not run together.

In a 3-quart bowl, heat water for 45 seconds or until it comes to a rolling boil. Stir in sugar, corn syrup, and butter. Cook on high (600–700 watts) 7–9 minutes, stirring once, or until candy thermometer registers 270–280°F. If using a microwave candy thermometer, it may be left in the oven. If using a regular candy thermometer, test mixture out of the oven.

Add flavoring and food coloring, if desired. Allow syrup to cool slightly. Working quickly, pour syrup onto upper end of each lollipop stick. It will shape itself into a circle. Allow to cool, then remove from sheet. When completely cool, wrap each lollipop in cellophane.

MAKES ABOUT 15 LOLLIPOPS

ROCKY ROAD

Here is a recipe from my article in Bon Appetit.

3 12-ounce packages semisweet real
   chocolate chips
3 ounces (3 squares) unsweetened baking
   chocolate, broken into pieces
9 tablespoons solid vegetable shortening
40 large marshmallows
2 cups whole roasted almonds

Grease deep casserole dish or a 1½- to 2-quart soufflé dish. Combine 1 package chocolate chips, 1 ounce baking chocolate, and 3 tablespoons shortening in 1-quart measuring cup and cook on high (600–700 watts) for 2 minutes. Stir until smooth. Pour into prepared dish. Sprinkle with half of the marshmallows and half of the nuts. Repeat operation, again using 1 package chocolate chips, 1 ounce baking chocolate, and 3 tablespoons shortening. Cover with remainder of marshmallows and nuts, and top with final layer of chocolate and shortening mixture. Allow to firm at room temperature before refrigerating. When firm and cool, cut into large pieces before serving.

MAKES ABOUT 4 POUNDS

CHOCOLATE CUPS

Because chocolate is so easy to work with in your micro-wave, I thought you might enjoy making and serving chocolate cups, which can then be filled with a white or chocolate mousse (see index for recipes). All you need for the cups is chocolate, foil cupcake liners, and some patience to wait until they set so you can remove the papers and admire your handiwork.

If you do not have time to make these, invite your teenagers to do it for you.

> **12 ounces milk chocolate or semisweet chocolate**
> **1 tablespoon vegetable shortening**
> **Paper cupcake pan liners**
> **2-inch or larger cupcake pan to fit paper liners**

Place chocolate in a 1-quart glass measure (if chocolate is in blocks, break into pieces). Add shortening. Melt on high (600–700 watts) for 1½–2 minutes, just until chocolate turns shiny (it will not melt until you stir). Stir until melted.

Set the pan liners in the cupcake pan. Spoon heated chocolate into the bottom of each paper cup. With the back of the spoon or a pastry brush, paint the chocolate up the sides, leaving ¼″ at top. Place in freezer until chocolate has hardened. Carefully pull away the foil cups. Fill with mousse, ice cream, or pie fillings and refrigerate. If filling with ice cream, freeze until ready to serve.

MAKES 18-24 CUPS

CHOCOLATE
BONBON CUPS

2 ounces semisweet chocolate, cut up
2 ounces milk chocolate, cut up

For this recipe, use a tiny bonbon case with a 7″ diameter, ⅝″ deep, plus tiny paper cases.

Place chocolates in a 1-cup glass measure and melt on high (600–700 watts) for 1–2 minutes, just until chocolate turns shiny. Stir until melted. Put the paper cases into the bonbon pan. Using a small pastry brush, paint a thin layer of melted chocolate on the bottom and sides of the paper liners to within ⅛″ of the rim. Place in freezer until chocolate has hardened. Remove paper cases from pan and carefully pull paper away from each chocolate cup.

MAKES ABOUT 30 CUPS

INDIAN CORN

Named because it resembles the Indian corn we now use only for decoration, it features fall colors and is appropriate for party favors when made into popcorn balls or shaped into a corn cob with a stick in the center to form a lollipop. When cold, it can be wrapped in plastic wrap and tied with colored ribbon.(See photo.)

> **2 tablespoons butter, divided**
> **1 cup whole natural almonds**
> **3 quarts popped corn**
> **1 cup dark raisins**
> **1 cup finely cut dried apricots**
> **1 cup firmly packed light brown sugar**
> **1 cup light corn syrup**
> **⅓ cup evaporated milk**
> **⅛ teaspoon salt**

Combine 1 tablespoon of the butter and the almonds in a shallow pie pan. Cook on high (600–700 watts) 3–4 minutes, until slightly toasted, stirring twice, to make certain almonds are coated with butter.

Combine popped corn, raisins, almonds, and apricots in large bowl and set aside. In a 4-quart bowl, combine sugar, corn syrup, evaporated milk, remaining butter, and salt. Cook on high 5 minutes. Stir until sugar is dissolved. Continue to cook on high until syrup reaches 234°F (soft ball stage) on candy thermometer, about 7–10 minutes.

Pour over popped corn mixture and, with two forks, mix lightly to coat ingredients. Let cool 5 minutes. Coat palms of hands with butter, then form mixture into oblong shapes, like ears of corn, or popcorn balls. Cool on waxed paper. When cool, push pointed end of wooden skewer into one end of each corn cob to form a handle, lollipop fashion. If preferred, mixture can be cooled until firm, then broken into chunks for eating.

MAKES 12–14 EARS OF CORN OR 10 LARGE POPCORN BALLS

Fruit Sauce
Cranberry Sauce
Homemade Yogurt
Golden Maple Syrup
Kahlua Fudge Topping
Kahlua Butterscotch Topping
Caramel Sauce
Thick Ginger Marmalade
Orange Marmalade
The Ultimate Chocolate Frosting
Rocky Road Frosting
Cream Cheese Frosting
Chocolate Leaves
Chocolate Curls

8
SAUCES, TOPPINGS, AND GARNISHES

While attending a chocolate workshop conducted by a famous French pastry chef, I was amazed when he arrived with a double boiler to hold the chocolate. The temperature was adjusted often and the chocolate stirred constantly throughout the demonstration. When the workshop was over, I asked the chef if he had ever considered using a microwave to melt the chocolate without the bother of a double boiler. Winking, he replied, "Shhh . . . that's how we do it in the restaurant."

The need for a double boiler and constant stirring is eliminated when making sauces in the microwave. The sauce is not in contact with a burner, so it will not burn. Stirring in a microwave is sometimes done just for the added insurance of a creamy, smooth sauce. A measuring cup is invaluable, for you can measure, mix, and cook in the same bowl.

Prepare sauces and toppings ahead and refrigerate. When ready to use, bring out of refrigerator and save a bit of time by letting them come to room temperature before heating (cold foods do not heat as quickly). Use medium (300–350 watts) to reheat. For ½ cup, start with 1 minute and add more time as needed. If reheating a topping, you may wish to use an attractive microwave pitcher.

Sauces and Toppings

FRUIT SAUCE

In response to the consumer's awareness that eating fruit with an overload of sugar does not necessarily mean a better-tasting product, I was delighted to discover packages of fresh fruit, fast-frozen to maintain quality control, without sugar, now being distributed all over the country. I use them for fruit pies when summer fruit is out of season or for delicious fruit sauces that can go over ice cream, pound cake, or baked apples. They are an excellent source of dessert sauces for those on sugar-free diets.

These sauces use a liqueur to make them a bit special. When I prepare sauces for family serving, I leave it out. Children also enjoy the fresh fruit flavor over puddings and ice cream, more than the overly sweet toppings.

Other fruits may be used, such as raspberries with raspberry liqueur, cherries with kirsch, peaches with amaretto, or whatever your favorite fruit might suggest.

When fresh fruit is used, the cooking time will be shorter, since the timing we use is for frozen fruit. If using the same amount of fruit (about 2 cups), use the same ingredients, start with 4–5 minutes of cooking time, and increase if necessary, cooking just until mixture is thickened.

½ cup sugar (may be reduced to ¼ cup)
1½ tablespoons cornstarch
½ cup water
1 12-ounce bag frozen unsweetened
   blueberries
2 tablespoons Grand Marnier liqueur
   (optional)

Combine sugar and cornstarch in an 8-cup glass measure. Blend in water until cornstarch is dissolved. Stir in berries. Cook on high (600–700 watts) 7–9 minutes, just until mixture is thickened, stirring once. Stir in liqueur, if desired. Serve warm or chilled.

MAKES ABOUT 2 CUPS

CRANBERRY SAUCE

If you prefer a thick sauce, similar to the canned cranberry sauce in the markets, you will enjoy this version, which uses a touch of cornstarch to thicken the natural cranberry juices.

It will be rather tart because I have cut the sugar content. Increase the sugar to suit your taste buds.

I like to cut 4 large oranges in half, scoop out the centers, and cut the edges in a zigzag pattern with a small sharp knife and fill them with the thickened, cooled sauce. The servings can be sprinkled with chopped nuts in season—a festive presentation! The cut-out orange centers may be cut into small pieces and added to the already cooked cranberry sauce.

 3 cups fresh cranberries
 ⅓ cup water
 ½ cup sugar
 1 tablespoon cornstarch
 2 tablespoons water

Combine cranberries, ⅓ cup water, and the sugar in a 2-quart glass measure. Stir well. Cook on high (600–700 watts) 6–7 minutes, until berries open. In a separate bowl, dissolve cornstarch in 2 tablespoons water. Stir into the cranberry mixture. Cook on high about 2 minutes, until mixture is clear and thick. Allow to cool before serving. Stores well, covered, in the refrigerator.

SERVES 4–6

HOMEMADE YOGURT

All you need is a starter. You can purchase plain yogurt (not diet) at your market and do it yourself if your microwave has a probe.

We like to add our own fresh fruit, which is cooked in the microwave in its own juices. You won't believe it is good for you because it tastes so good.

> 1⅓ cups nonfat dry milk
> **Water**
> 1⅓ cups whole milk
> 1 12-ounce can evaporated milk
> ⅓ cup plain yogurt

Combine dry milk and enough water to make 2 cups milk in a 2-quart bowl. Stir until dry milk is dissolved, then add the whole milk.

Insert temperature probe into center. Set probe to 190°F. Cook on high (600–700 watts) to 190°F, about 8 minutes. Remove from microwave and blend in the evaporated milk. Allow it to cool to 115°F.

Blend a small amount of the milk mixture into the yogurt. Stir yogurt into milk. Insert probe into center of mixture. Cover with plastic wrap. Plug in probe and cook on medium low (200–250 watts) (defrost) for 3 hours. You may need to reset your probe every hour to keep it at 115°F. Check the readout on your display. Set aside for 1 hour before chilling in refrigerator.

MAKES ABOUT 4 CUPS

GOLDEN MAPLE SYRUP

Many years ago, when our children were very young, we drove for two hours to visit a favorite sister-in-law who was anxiously awaiting our arrival in the kitchen with a batch of aromatic pancakes. Her three youngsters greeted us at the door with "Our mommy makes her own maple syrup!" For some reason, I felt like an unfit mother. So naturally, I asked for the recipe.

It is so easy in the microwave and so inexpensive, and you can tell your children you made it yourself!

> 1 cup water
> 1 pound brown sugar
> ½ teaspoon maple flavoring or to taste

Place water in a 2-quart glass measure. Cook on high (600–700 watts) 3 minutes. Stir in sugar. Continue to cook on high for about 2–3 minutes, just until sugar is dissolved. Stir in flavoring.

Pour into pitcher and serve warm. May be stored, covered. We always pour what we think we need for breakfast in a glass or ceramic pitcher and heat in the microwave for about 1 minute. It's delicious over vanilla ice cream, too.

MAKES ABOUT 2 CUPS

KAHLUA FUDGE TOPPING

1 cup unsweetened cocoa powder
⅔ cup granulated sugar
½ cup packed light brown sugar
1 cup whipping cream
¼ cup Kahlua
½ cup butter
1½ teaspoons vanilla

Place cocoa and sugars in a 2-quart glass measure. Stir in cream and Kahlua and add butter. Cook on high (600–700 watts) 2 minutes. Stir well and continue to cook 2 minutes. Stir in vanilla. Allow to cool. Store in covered jar in refrigerator.

This is best served warm. To reheat, heat on medium (300–350 watts) for 2–4 minutes.

MAKES ABOUT 2¾ CUPS

KAHLUA BUTTERSCOTCH

This tasty topping may be made ahead, stored in the refrigerator, and reheated as needed. It complements puddings, ice cream, crepes, pancakes, and waffles.

1 cup packed light brown sugar
½ cup dark corn syrup
½ cup whipping cream
¼ cup butter
¼ cup Kahlua
1½ teaspoons vanilla

Combine sugar, corn syrup, cream, butter, Kahlua, and vanilla in a 2-quart glass measure. Cook on high (600–700 watts) 5–7 minutes, stirring twice.

To reheat, use medium (300–350 watts) for 2–4 minutes, depending on the amount of topping you are heating.

Variation: Add ⅓ cup finely chopped toasted macadamia nuts, almonds, filberts, or pecans before cooling.

MAKES ABOUT 2 CUPS

CARAMEL SAUCE

A rich caramel sauce thickened with melted marshmallows and flavored with Kahlua. May be stored in a covered jar in your refrigerator and reheated before using. Serve it over apple pie slices, ice cream, or chocolate cake.

¼ **cup Kahlua**
1 **cup whipping cream**
1¼ **cups packed light brown sugar**
3 **cups miniature marshmallows**
¼ **cup (½ stick) butter**
1½ **teaspoons vanilla**

Combine Kahlua, cream, sugar, and marshmallows in a 2-quart glass measure. Cook on high (600–700 watts) for 9–10 minutes, stirring once or twice. A candy thermometer should register 224°F. Add butter and vanilla. Allow to cool and store in refrigerator.

To reheat, use medium (300–350 watts) for 2–3 minutes.

MAKES ABOUT 2¼ CUPS

THICK GINGER MARMALADE

Fresh ginger is one of nature's great gifts. I find I am always attracted to recipes using ginger, probably because I can remember my mother spending hours making a ginger candy for a holiday celebration every year. Knowing how much I loved the flavor, she would always spoon off the top of the ginger/honey mixture as it cooked in a huge pot on the stove and let me taste.

When Associated Press food writer Cecily Brownstone printed a recipe for Thick Ginger Marmalade in her column in the Los Angeles Times, *I placed it on my pile of recipes. I like to convert recipes to the microwave that read "stir constantly" because it is never necessary to do that in the microwave. Even though the cooking time may not always be shorter, the luxury of cooking without constant supervision makes microwave recipes worthwhile.*

For ginger lovers, it is definitely worth the time required to precook the fresh ginger with changes of water. This marmalade is thick, delicious, and stores well in your refrigerator. For long storage, it should be preserved in sterile glass jars with proper lids.

If I find I have more than I can use, I share with fellow ginger lovers by wrapping the jar in an attractive napkin, pulling the corners up over the lid, and tying the napkin with a colorful ribbon. Great gift for holiday giving.

    1 pound (approximately) fresh gingerroot
    2 tablespoons lemon juice
    1 ¾-ounce package powdered fruit pectin
    5 cups sugar

Using a swivel-blade peeler, remove outer skin from gingerroot and cut ginger into 1-inch-thick slices. Place in a 5-quart casserole and fill ¾ full with cold water. Cook on high (600–700 watts) 25 minutes (it should boil for 15 minutes and will take about 10 minutes to reach boiling point). Drain ginger in colander. Return to casserole and fill ¾ full with cold water. Cook on high until ginger is tender-crisp and can be pierced with a fork, about 45 minutes. Let stand, covered, about 10 minutes. Drain in colander, return to casserole, and fill ¾ full with fresh cold water. Let stand 15 minutes, then drain well.

In food processor or by hand, chop ginger until it is the size of rice grains. (I leave mine a little thicker for additional texture.) Do not puree.

You should have about 2½ cups of chopped ginger. Place it in the casserole. Add 1 cup cold water, lemon juice, and fruit pectin. Cook on high until mixture comes to a full boil, about 5 minutes. Immediately stir in all sugar. Continue cooking on high until it again reaches a rolling boil. Allow it to boil hard for a full minute.

Remove from microwave and use metal spoon to skim off any foam that might appear on the top.

Immediately ladle into hot clean jars, leaving ¼ inch space at top. With a damp cloth, wipe jar rims and threads clean. If you plan to store jars, follow directions on pectin packages. Jars should then be covered with hot paraffin and sealed with hot lids, etc., as directed.

If, like me, you are not into making preserves and do not have the necessary equipment, you can still enjoy the marmalade by filling clean jars almost full, covering with their proper lids, and storing in the refrigerator. I have found it stores well for several months. It can also be frozen.

MAKES ABOUT 5 CUPS

ORANGE MARMALADE

Once you taste this easy-to-prepare marmalade, you will never again ask why you should bother when you can buy a jar in your market.

I find that several jars will last in my refrigerator for several weeks and I make my friends and neighbors happy by sharing this thick, delectable jam with them. We eat it with toast or crackers or on ice cream as a dessert topping.

> 3 medium oranges
> 3 medium lemons
> 1½ cups water
> ¼ teaspoon baking soda
> 5 cups sugar
> 3 ounces liquid fruit pectin

Peel oranges and lemons, removing white membrane between sections. Cut fruit into pieces on plate so that you do not lose the juices. Place fruit and juices in a 5-quart casserole. Add water and baking soda. Stir. Cover and cook on high (600–700 watts) 25 minutes, stirring once or twice.

Stir in sugar. Bring to a full rolling boil and allow it to boil hard for 2 minutes. Remove from microwave and stir in liquid pectin. If any foam appears, skim with metal spoon. Allow to cool. At this point, you may pour into hot sterilized jars or place in jars to refrigerate.

MAKES ABOUT 5 CUPS

Frostings

THE ULTIMATE
CHOCOLATE FROSTING

I did not name this frosting, but it is well deserved. Easy to prepare with your mixer—no cooking involved, but I thought it was too good to leave out. After all, good taste and a minimum of effort are what this book is all about!

6 tablespoons butter or margarine
¾ cup unsweetened cocoa powder
3½ cups confectioners' (powdered) sugar
6–7 tablespoons milk
1 teaspoon vanilla

In small bowl with mixer at medium speed, beat butter to soften. Add cocoa and confectioners' sugar alternately with 6 tablespoons of the milk. Beat until it is spreading consistency (do not underbeat), adding an additional tablespoon of milk if needed. (I found I needed to add it.) Blend in the vanilla. Spread on cake with rubber spatula.

MAKES ABOUT 2¾ CUPS (ENOUGH FOR A 2-LAYER CAKE
OR A LARGE BUNDT CAKE)

ROCKY ROAD FROSTING

A chocolate marshmallow cream frosting for any cake.

2 1-ounce squares unsweetened chocolate
2 cups miniature marshmallows, divided
¼ cup milk
¼ cup (½ stick) butter
2 cups confectioners' (powdered) sugar,
    sifted if lumpy
1 teaspoon vanilla
½ cup sliced toasted almonds

Combine chocolate, 1 cup marshmallows, milk, and butter in a 2-quart bowl. Cook on high (600–700 watts) 1½ minutes. Stir well. Add sugar and vanilla. Using an electric mixer, beat until it is smooth and thick enough to spread. Stir in the remaining cup of marshmallows and the nuts.

MAKES ENOUGH FOR A 9″ LAYER CAKE OR A BUNDT CAKE

CREAM CHEESE FROSTING

Complements carrot cakes and zucchini cakes.

1 8-ounce package cream cheese, softened
¼ cup (½ stick) butter, softened
2 teaspoons vanilla
2 cups confectioners' (powdered) sugar
1 tablespoon grated lemon rind

Whip cream cheese until smooth. Add butter and whip thoroughly. Stir in remaining ingredients and mix until well blended.

MAKES ENOUGH FROSTING FOR
A 2-LAYER CAKE OR A 9″ BUNDT CAKE

Garnishes

CHOCOLATE LEAVES

Used to garnish cakes and desserts, these are quite easy to make. Leaves from the garden are used to form them with melted chocolate. The best leaves to use are those with waxy or thick surfaces with prominent veins. For example, use fresh camellia, rose, ivy, holly, or any similar nonpoisonous leaves.

The leaves can also be made with white chocolate. Prepare some of each and overlap white and chocolate leaves alternately in a circle on top of a round cake or torte.

> **4 ounces semisweet chocolate or white chocolate**
> **24 nonpoisonous leaves**

Place chocolate in a 1-cup glass measure. Melt on high (600–700 watts) for 1–2 minutes, just until the chocolate turns shiny (it will not melt until you stir).

Using a spoon, generously coat the underside of each leaf with chocolate, holding the leaf by its stem end and being careful not to let the chocolate run onto the top of the leaf. With your fingertip, wipe the edges of the leaf to remove any excess chocolate. Place leaves on a plate, chocolate side up, and refrigerate until firm. Then separate chocolate from each leaf by gently peeling leaf away, starting with stem end.

Leaves can be stored for several weeks in a refrigerator or freezer in an airtight container.

MAKES 24 LEAVES

CHOCOLATE CURLS

1 frozen chocolate bar

Draw a potato peeler across the top of the frozen chocolate bar to make thin curls. Use to garnish cakes and other desserts.

Eggnog
Eggnog Fluff
Sangria
Irish Coffee
Cappuccino
Mexican Hot Chocolate

9
BEVERAGES

When we think of drinks in the microwave, it is usually to reheat a cup of coffee. There are many other ways to put the microwave to work for you: prepare a syrup for a cool and refreshing sangria, an Irish coffee, a Mexican hot chocolate, or a rich and foamy eggnog before your guests arrive, and chill until ready to serve. Because the microwave timer goes off automatically, nothing is boiling over on the stove while you are busy enjoying company or family. What a help during the rush of entertaining!

Some insights for heating liquids:

The ideal utensil is, of course, the wonderful glass measure with handles (the familiar glass measuring cup). On high power (600–700 watts), it will take between 2½ and 3 minutes to bring 1 cup liquid to a boil. It does not take double the amount of time for 2 cups, but about 1½ times as long.

Milk boils quickly, just as it does on a cooktop, so one should watch carefully. If you have large amounts of milk, bring it almost to a boil on high, then reduce to medium to prevent a boilover if the recipe calls for continued cooking.

EGGNOG

A rich, cooked eggnog that can be made ahead for guests at holiday time. It is simply a rich custard that is easy to make in your microwave. Remember, for best results, use a whisk to beat egg yolks and milk frequently to keep the custard light and fluffy, without lumps. Save the egg whites for meringue recipes.

3 cups milk
⅔ cup sugar
8 egg yolks
1 cup rum or brandy
½ teaspoon vanilla
Ground cinnamon for garnish
Whipped cream for garnish (optional)

Combine milk and sugar in a 2-quart glass measure. Cook on high (600–700 watts) for 10–12 minutes or just until boiling. Continue to cook on medium (300–350 watts) for 5 minutes, stirring twice. Meanwhile, beat egg yolks until thick and lemon-colored (about 5 minutes), using an electric mixer. Gradually stir about 1 cup of the hot milk into egg yolks. Return egg mixture to hot milk. Whisk well. Continue to cook on medium for 2–3 minutes, until thickened, stirring 3 times. Stir in rum or brandy and vanilla. Pour into 12 individual serving glasses and chill. Sprinkle with cinnamon before serving and place a dollop of whipped cream on top if desired.

Variation: You may also whip the 8 egg whites with ¼ cup sugar just before serving and garnish the eggnog with a heaping spoonful of freshly made meringue.

MAKES TWELVE 4-OUNCE SERVINGS

EGGNOG FLUFF

Too bad we think of eggnog only at holiday time—this one can be habit-forming.

12 egg yolks
1¼ cups sugar, divided
4 cups milk, divided
12 egg whites
1 cup whipping cream
2 tablespoons vanilla
1½ cups amaretto (almond liqueur)
Freshly grated nutmeg

In a medium mixing bowl, beat egg yolks until thick and smooth. In a 2-quart glass measure, combine egg yolks, ¾ cup sugar, and ¾ cup milk. Blend well. Cook on medium (300–350 watts) 5–7 minutes, until mixture thickens to a soft custard, stirring frequently with wire whisk. Set aside to cool.

In a large mixing bowl, beat egg whites until frothy. Slowly add remaining ½ cup sugar. Beat until soft peaks form. Making certain the custard is completely cooled, fold it into the egg whites. In a medium bowl, whip cream until stiff. Add whipped cream, remaining milk, and vanilla to custard. Fold gently until blended. Refrigerate several hours or overnight.

To serve, stir gently but well and add liqueur. Sprinkle with nutmeg. Ladle from a bowl into individual glass cups.

MAKES 14–16 SERVINGS

SANGRIA

A popular Spanish red wine punch that has become world famous. It is a delightfully refreshing drink, especially in warm weather.

　　¼ **cup sugar**
　　1 cup water
　　1 bottle full-bodied red wine
　　½ **teaspoon orange bitters**
　　1 orange, sliced thin
　　1 lemon or lime, sliced thin

In a 1-quart glass measure, combine sugar and water. Cook on high (600–700 watts) 3–4 minutes, stirring once, until sugar is completely dissolved. Allow to cool.

Mix the sugar syrup with the wine and bitters in a punch bowl. Add the orange and lemon slices. Chill, then add ice cubes and serve.

MAKES 8-10 SERVINGS

IRISH COFFEE

This traditional beverage combines coffee with a jigger of whiskey, and the first taste sensation is masked by the sugar and whipped cream—but it has a kick!

　　2½ **cups water**
　　¼ **cup instant coffee crystals**
　　4 jiggers (1½ ounces each) Irish whiskey
　　4 teaspoons sugar
　　Whipped cream for garnish (optional)

Place water in a 1-quart glass measure. Cook on high (600–700 watts) until boiling (about 6 minutes). Stir in coffee crystals until dissolved. Measure whiskey into 4 stemmed glasses. Add 1 teaspoon sugar to each glass. Place metal spoo in glass to prevent glass from breaking and pour hot coffee on.o metal spoon. Repeat with each glass. Stir. Top with whipped cream. Serve immediately.

MAKES 4 SERVINGS

CAPPUCCINO

For coffee and chocolate lovers, this is a combination of both with a touch of brandy to bring you warmth on a cold, brisk evening. If you travel to the snow for weekends, throw your microwave into the car. It can be a tremendous money saver to prepare easy snacks in your room—or even breakfast, lunch, and dinner. Just take plenty of paper plates, some of the heavy-duty kind now available for cooking, serving, and storing. To keep your perishables cold, an insulated cold box will hold overnight—or you can place them outside in nature's refrigerator.

> **2 cups milk**
> **¼ cup semisweet chocolate chips**
> **2 teaspoons instant coffee**
> **8 tablespoons brandy**
> **Whipped cream for garnish (optional)**
> **2 teaspoons sugar (optional)**

Combine milk and chocolate in a 1-quart glass measure. Cook on high (600–700 watts) 3–4 minutes, until hot; do not allow it to boil. Stir in coffee and stir until dissolved. Divide among 4 mugs. Stir 2 tablespoons brandy into each mug. Top with whipped cream and serve immediately.

Add sugar to the milk if you would like a sweeter drink. The chocolate has sugar in it, and for some that is enough. You can always stir in the sugar at the end to your taste.

MAKES 4 SERVINGS

MEXICAN
HOT CHOCOLATE

Mexican cuisine is rich in tradition, and this beverage is one example. When the weather turns cool and snow is on the ground, chocolate and cinnamon are mixed for a delicious and satisfying drink.

6 cups milk
½ cup sugar
3 1-ounce squares unsweetened baking chocolate
6 inches stick cinnamon
2 eggs, beaten
1 teaspoon vanilla
6 cinnamon sticks for garnish
Whipped cream for garnish (optional)

In a 3-quart casserole, combine milk, sugar, chocolate, and 6 inches of stick cinnamon. Cook on high (600–700 watts) for 10–12 minutes, stirring 3 times, until chocolate melts and milk is close to boiling. Slowly stir 1 cup of hot mixture into beaten eggs and return it to the casserole.

Continue to cook on medium (300–350 watts) for 3 minutes. Remove cinnamon stick. Add vanilla. Beat with rotary beater until frothy. Pour into mugs and garnish with additional cinnamon sticks. If desired, add a dollop of whipped cream to each mug just before serving. The heat of the milk will melt it quickly.

MAKES SIX 8-OUNCE SERVINGS

ABOUT THE AUTHOR

Popularly regarded as "the mother of microwave cooking," Thelma Pressman is known both for her cooking expertise and her microwave innovations. She is president and founder of the Microwave Cooking Center and a respected designer of microwave cookware and products, having created many designs used in the market today. As director of consumer education and services for Sanyo Electric, Inc., Ms. Pressman counts among her responsibilities a close involvement with cookbook development. At present, Ms. Pressman is consultant to *Bon Appetit,* where she served as columnist for three years. While associate director of the *International Microwave Institute Journal,* she created the Cooking Appliance Section of the International Microwave Power Institute and served on the international educational council for setting standards for microwave manufacturers.

Ms. Pressman is a popular spokesperson for the microwave industry and appears frequently on TV and radio programs. She has written more than seventy articles, which have appeared in

House and Garden, House Beautiful, Bon Appetit, Woman's Day, Microwave Magazine, and *California Living.* Her bestselling book, *The Art of Microwave Cooking,* is published by Contemporary Books.

Ms. Pressman resides in Encino, California, with her husband Mo.

INDEX

155